"As an accomplished business leader, Whitney Johnson acutely understands how to translate ambitions into action. *Dare, Dream, Do* not only ignites the courage to pursue your aspirations, but also serves as a powerful guide to achieve what once may have seemed out of reach."

—Moira Forbes, publisher *ForbesWoman*

"Whitney Johnson maps out a masterpiece for women that is filled with wisdom, strategies, fascinating stories, and all that matters most in life. She takes us on a journey as we learn to express our dreams, embrace our powers, and expand our hearts. *Dare, Dream, Do* is an incredible book. I want to give this book to every woman I know."

—Lolly Daskal, president and founder of Lead From Within:
Heart -based Leadership for Work and Life

"Whether you are just setting off on the journey to adulthood, making a career transition, nurturing a family, or looking for meaning in an empty nest, *Dare, Dream, Do* will inspire you. And whether your dream is to start an orphanage, a dress company, or a family of eight, you'll find your story here. Don't know what your dream is? Whitney Johnson gives you the tools to dig it out, 'date' it, commit to it, and make it happen. I love this book! I'll be sending it to just about every woman I know."

—Wendy Ulrich, founder of Sixteen Stones Center for Growth,
partner at the RBL Group, and co-author of *The Why of Work*

"With this beautiful and inspiring book, Whitney Johnson will make you a believer in dreams again. She shows us how they help shape life's meaning, and why dreams are a practical necessity when it comes to reaching your fullest potential. The key is figuring out how to turn those dreams into reality—and *Dare, Dream, Do* is the roadmap you've been looking for."

—Heidi Grant Halvorson, associate director of The Motivation
Science Center, Columbia Business School, and author of
Succeed and *Nine Things Successful People Do Differently*

"Every woman, regardless of age or profession, should read *Dare, Dream, Do*. Through stories of real women, their dreams and their struggles, Johnson's book has created an instant community. What's more, she has opened the door for women to empower themselves to dare, dream, and do."

—Joanne Wilson, angel investor, The Gotham Gal, and co-founder of the Women's Entrepreneur Festival

"Wow. Right from Whitney Johnson's heart directly on to the pages of *Dare, Dream, Do*. Read this important book today. It will inspire you to become the gatekeeper of your own dreams and take personal control of achieving them. Johnson's passion is compelling. It's worth daring to be great."

—Saul Kaplan, founder and chief catalyst, Business Innovation Factory

"*Dare, Dream, Do* belongs in every success toolkit. Business leader and master storyteller, Whitney Johnson shows how remarkable things happen when we dare to claim our strengths, own our dreams, and do what we're meant to do. A fabulous guide for business and for life."

—Liz Strauss, international business strategist and author of *Successful-Blog.com*

"As a lifelong dreamer, I was immediately intrigued (and even moved to tears) by Whitney Johnson's observations that women feel it isn't their privilege to dream, and that most people don't dream well in isolation. In this book, Johnson inspires a shift in mindset to resolve these two problems. She makes a case for the importance of dreaming and equips readers with the reflective fodder to identify their dreams and bring them to fruition via elegant prose, insightful questions, community-driven stories, and Johnson's own intriguing personal history. Whether you're trying to identify your dream, forge a new path, or confirm that you're on the right one, *Dare, Dream, Do* will inspire you to rock your personal space and also think beyond it—whether that means paying it forward, creating collaborative teams, or showing your children how to dream."

—Christine Koh, neuroscientist turned writer, editor, designer, and digital strategist (ChristineKoh.com)

"Dare, Dream, Do is a well of wisdom, strategy, and shared personal experiences of women who have overcome the mundane by choosing to dream, and living to dream. Motivated by her own learned sense of dreaming and seeking her own passions, Whitney convinces women that dreaming isn't senseless, but that it's actually necessary for purposeful living. She offers both motivation and a strategy for coming out of our shells and doing what we were meant to do. . . . and truly gifted to do. *Dare, Dream, Do* is the sideline coach we all need to see that our secret wants and dreams are realized.

—Sarah Wright, children's book illustrator and textile designer, Sarah Jane Studios

"Read this book for your soul and read it for your future! Join Whitney on an inspired journey toward realizing the power and potential in yourself. Relish in the magnificent and wise reflections of strong women who are living their dreams and being their best. Learn how to catalog your talents and channel them toward a thrilling future. Then start dreaming BIG."

—Betsy Morgan, former CEO, *The Huffington Post*, and president of The Blaze

"Whitney Johnson has crafted a wonderful, eloquent, and accessible step-by-step prescriptive on how to uncork the bottomless bottle of hidden dreams. *Dare, Dream, Do* is a manual on how to dream big, rightsizing your dream, and recognizing the potential within. It helps us understand that in order to find who we are, we must step up and step out, discovering what we are meant to do and what our story is meant to be. Whitney's tour de force captures architect Daniel Burnham's imperative: 'Make no little plans. They have no magic to stir men's blood.' Dream big today, and bigger tomorrow."

—Craig Hatkoff, founder of the Tribeca Film Festival, and
co-author of the *New York Times* bestseller, *Owen and Mzee*

"Inspiring and honest, **Dare, Dream, Do** really touched me. For someone who grew up with a single mother in a small town in Finland and got through the ranks of the highly competitive American fashion industry, hanging on to one's inner dreams is a must. Whitney writes in a straightforward engaging way and analyzes the wonderful magic of believing in your dreams. *Dare, Dream, Do* is a book that I would highly recommend for anyone in the beginning of their careers, or in the middle wondering if they are realizing their full potential in life."

—Johanna Uurasjarvi, creative director, Leifsdottir,
former creative director, Anthropologie

"Dare, Dream, Do is filled with great advice and energizing true stories from real women who are bootstrapping their way toward a dream. Pick up this book and you just might find yourself living a life you've only imagined! This should be required reading for anyone with a forgotten wish, a pie-in-the-sky fantasy, or a quiet dream hidden in their heart. In other words—everyone."

—Barbara Corcoran, NYC real estate mogul and
investor on ABC's reality show *Shark Tank*

"It is rare to encounter someone with a seemingly magical ability to help so many people achieve their dreams. Whitney Johnson is one of those people. On every page of she invites you to dare, dream, and then do. Truly, she is a dream whisperer."

—Jane Clayson Johnson, Emmy award-
winning journalist and author

Dare, Dream, Do

Remarkable Things Happen
when you Dare *to* Dream

WHITNEY JOHNSON

First published by Bibliomotion, Inc.
33 Manchester Road
Brookline, MA 02446
Tel: 617-934-2427
www.bibliomotion.com

10 9 8 7 6 5 4 3 2

Printed in the United States of America
ISBN 978-1-937134-12-9

Library of Congress Control Number: 2012932637

CONTENTS

INTRODUCTION

I sincerely doubt that anyone who knew me as a child or even a teenager would classify me as a dreamer. I certainly didn't see myself as one.

The oldest of four children, I grew up in San Jose, California, long before San Jose was Silicon Valley. At age eighteen, I enrolled in college with plans to major in music but with no real sense of what I would do after graduation, other than anticipating I would eventually marry and have children.

By the time I graduated nine years later (I'd left school for three years to make money and do missionary work in South America) I had married. Upon graduation, and two years into our marriage, my husband and I moved to New York City so he could study molecular biology at Columbia University. Because his PhD program was going to take five to seven years and provided only a small stipend, I had to earn a living. I decided I wanted to do that as a professional, working in an office. There was just one problem: I had no business experience. Being a twenty-seven-year-old woman with little more than an undergraduate degree in music, I pursued work as a secretary. After about a month of looking, I landed a job as a sales assistant to a retail broker at Smith Barney.

Although I now had a job, I still didn't know what I wanted to be when I grew up. Yet, as I watched the Ivy League–trained professionals I worked with, most of whom were hugely successful men, they didn't seem any smarter than I was. I wanted to do what they were doing. If I had to work, I wanted a real job, a career—one that was challenging *and* lucrative. "I may not have a degree from Princeton, and I may not be an engineer, but I can be successful on Wall Street," I told myself.

THE GATEKEEPER OF YOUR DREAMS

When I was an undergraduate, I attended an information session about law school. I was intrigued by a law degree, but dismissed it as a pipe dream. I wasn't sure I was smart enough or that it was my right to even try.

There are many reasons why people don't dare to dream. When I was in college, my parents were still the gatekeepers of my dreams; they told me what I could or couldn't do, including weighing in on who I should marry. By age twenty-seven, I was the gatekeeper of my dreams. Being thrown into a vibrant new place (New York City) and having a supportive husband enabled me to see myself in a different context; but perhaps the most powerful motivator was that there was a pressing need. With my husband's graduate studies and post-doctoral work expected to last at least a decade, low-paying secretarial work would have us living at the poverty level until our late thirties.

Those first steps along the path to my first big career dream were rocky. Without the skills, a relevant degree, or, most importantly, confidence, I was starting from behind. But I threw myself into my sales assistant job, took business courses at night, and in early 1992, three years after arriving in New York, my big break came. I was working at Nomura Securities, and my boss, Cesar Baez, promoted me to investment banking analyst. He took a chance and bridged for me what is often an unbridgeable divide between secretary and professional.

After a seven-year stint in banking, and the birth of our first child, I moved to sell-side research, first at Salomon Smith Barney then at Merrill Lynch. As a sell-side research analyst, I built detailed financial-valuation models, crafted investment theses, and made stock calls. When I took a sabbatical from Wall Street in order to pursue new dreams, I was widely considered to be an expert on the stocks under my coverage, and I had earned a double ranking in the *Institutional Investor* survey, a poll conducted among the world's largest professional money managers; I was rated number one in Latin American media and number two in Latin American telecoms.

THE POWER OF SHARING

After daring and dreaming for more than a decade in New York, we moved to Boston for my husband's work, and I began to see that dreaming is a process. I came to recognize that achieving goals isn't as much about gaining credentials or training as it is believing in possibilities and being in a place where you can explore possibilities. I also confirmed that necessity *is* the mother of invention.

To my surprise, when I asked women what they dreamed of doing, many responded, "I don't have a dream" or "I don't know that my dreams are within reach." Many felt that it wasn't their privilege to dream. This concerned me. These were highly educated, eminently capable women who are the bedrock of our society. I saw so many possibilities for these women. I knew I had to do something—and that something was creating the *Dare to Dream* blog (daretodream.typepad.com) a safe spare where intelligent, articulate women could explore their dormant dreams.

DREAMS OF ANY SHAPE AND SIZE

Maybe your dream is to marry a good man and raise a happy family, or to become a doctor, an artist, a teacher, to run your own business. Perhaps your dream will be to run a marathon, learn to knit, sing in public, or run for political office. Maybe it's to make your corner of the world one where everyone wants to be. Whether you are pursuing one dream or many, are still discovering your dreams, or are just beginning to explore what it means to dream, I hope this book will be an inspiration and a guide.

Dare, Dream, Do is divided into three parts:

- Part 1: Dare: Why Dreaming Is Essential
- Part 2: Dream: Boldly Finding Your Dreams
- Part 3: Do: Making Your Dreams Happen

Interwoven into the narrative are the stories of dozens of women; many of these women, ranging in age from twenty to seventy, initially shared their stories on the *Dare to Dream* blog. As I dared these women to grapple with the why, what, and how of their dreams, the richness of our *Dare to Dream* conversation increased exponentially. I learned that most of us don't dream well in isolation. Because the skills women bring to family, civic, and professional life are often intangible or overlooked, we need others to help us recognize what we're doing and give our dreams life. My friend Jen Thomas described her experience of reading this book on a flight, "Reading this manuscript (somewhere over Missouri) magically changed my solitary seat of 22B, into a room full of intelligent and inspiring women, all sharing their dreams and ideas."

SUIT UP AND SHOW UP

Life is full of lessons. One I learned in my early twenties, while working as a volunteer missionary in Uruguay, proved immensely valuable to my *Dare to Dream* pursuits. It's common practice among missionaries to pray that we'll find people who are interested in our message. Being thousands of miles from home, as my peers and I were in Uruguay, those prayers became pretty fervent because people often ignored us, or worse, slammed doors in our faces. That's why I found the words of one of our leaders, a Dutchman by the name of Jacob de Jager, both surprising and compelling. "Instead of praying that you'll find people, pray that they'll find you," he said. In other words, if we make grand plans, and get on with executing them, our dreams will find us. Suit up and show up. We might not learn to dream until we're grown—but if we show up, our dreams will too.

I dream best when I start simply. I encourage you to take a similar approach: begin reading this book, even a page or two at a time, scribble notes in the margins, mull over the ideas as you move through your day, notice the ideas that gently alight in your mind, act on one or two of them. Then repeat.

Regardless of the dream, we all start in the same place, a place of possibility, of seeing something that looks and feels so much bigger than we are or maybe believe we could ever be. That's why a dream is a dare. But we do it anyway, because dreaming matters—to our families, our communities, the world, and especially to ourselves. When we dream, remarkable things can happen.

Do you dare?

PART ONE

Dare
Why Dreaming Is Essential

Do not dare not to dare.

—C.S. Lewis, twentieth-
century British author

Dreaming is an inalienable right. We knew this as children. We believed we could be or do anything we imagined. Astronaut, Egyptologist, prima ballerina, mother of a dozen children, President of the United States—sure, why not? Unfortunately, as adults we often put our dearest dreams away, as life hands us unexpected challenges or circumstances and the harsh realities of economic necessity whittle away at our energy and our hopes. Dreaming truly becomes a dare.

This section is meant to underscore that dreaming is your privilege, and to outline why we must dream. When we dream we make meaning of life, discover the essence of ourselves, truly grow up, and most importantly, model for children how to dream. As you read the accounts of women who are wrestling with the dare of dreaming, you may want to give voice to your own story, and I encourage you to do so. The act of writing down our dreams allows us to own them and eventually act on them. As you recognize that dreaming is essential, your story will be woven into this tapestry of women's voices, who like you, are daring to dream.

1

TO MAKE MEANING OF LIFE

When I was seventeen, my parents divorced. In retrospect, it's not so much the divorce that was painful, it was everything that it meant—that my parents didn't really love each other, that maybe they never had (my mom was pregnant when they married), that they weren't happy. As their oldest child, I wondered if perhaps things might have been different if only I'd been brilliant enough or attractive enough. Or would they even have married if I hadn't been born?

Sharing those memories is still painful, even decades after the fact; but as I get older, I recognize that some of my greatest strengths were born of that sadness. For example, my desire to have a happy marriage and a happy family life is resolute. Period. (My household is far from perfect, but we're happy.) When someone I know is affected by a divorce, I understand. I know that the situation is complicated and that, regardless of why the marriage is dissolving, the experience is wrenching. My drive, my intense focus on improvement, is likely a means of trying to measure up, and I'm quite certain that my laser-like focus on encouraging and mentoring is my attempt to be the encouraging voice I wanted to hear.

Difficulties we don't deserve happen to all of us. Yet, when we dream, we begin to make meaning of these challenges. We give ourselves hope, and we can hope that the sorrow and pain we've walked through will help lighten someone else's load.

USING CHALLENGES AS A SPRINGBOARD

When there's something we want to accomplish, the power to achieve that dream often comes from facing our most wrenching sadness. That was certainly the case for Emily Orton, a schoolteacher turned stay-at-home mother in New York City.

Emily Orton: *Running Down a Dream*

By the time my daughter Lily was four months old she was showing signs of developmental delay. Despite reassurances from my midwife and my pediatrician, I wearied myself with inconclusive Internet research about Down syndrome.

My husband called me paranoid. Finally, when Lily was six months old, blood tests revealed the microscopic extra chromosome that shook our paradigm. There was some reeling and some relief. At least now I didn't have to worry *if* anything was wrong. I could get to work.

Genuine acceptance and resilient humor, two of my husband's hallmark qualities, buoyed us over the first few hours of transition. He wanted to make T-shirts that said, "*We put the O in Chromosome*" or "*I'm down with Down's.*" He talked of how our four older children would be jealous of the cool trips Lily would get to take with us in our wild retirement years.

Encouragement from friends and family enveloped us as a whirlwind of evaluations and a battery of medical tests ensued.

Through it all, I held my girl. I nuzzled her soft, warm head. I considered her future. So much was still uncertain, but I knew she would have to work hard for every achievement. I wanted to do something hard, too. The circumstances of my life aligned to make a marathon possible. I wanted to honor Lily by running a marathon.

I began training by taking the stairs instead of the elevator. I had worked up to ten miles with my friend Heather, who served as my trainer and partner, when Lily began having seizures. Finding a pediatric neurologist on a holiday weekend was a saga unto itself. The doctor interpreted the mass of EEG scribbles as electrical misfires in Lily's brain; she was swiftly admitted into the pediatric ward.

Lily obliged us by having a seizure shortly after being hooked up to the EEG and video monitors. She was immediately diagnosed with hypsarrhythmia. Lily was subjected to more tests than I ever took in college. I learned how to give injections to my infant. By day two of our hospital vigil, I needed to run. I knew I might have to give up the marathon, but my body needed to move. My husband took over the bedside duties while I cared for and held our other children, slept in my own bed, and ran with Heather. The crisp morning air, the steady rhythm of our tandem footfall, the oxygen, the endorphins, and the encouragement of my dear friend convinced me that, more than ever, I needed to run the marathon.

Lily came home and I continued training. The neurologist assured me that the chaotic electrical impulses in her brain weren't causing damage. She descended into a developmental pause. I ran. She became very fat. I ran. Her eyes were dull and unfocused. I ran. She never smiled. I ran. My husband and our four older children needed me, too. I ran.

Heather and I trained almost every day. On weekends a larger party formed for the long runs. Sometimes the conversation would transport me into the concerns and joys of the other women. The miles of quiet along the river were a sanctuary for my searching prayers. Often enough that Heather wasn't surprised, my voice would tremble, and the wind would send tears sliding sideways across my cheeks as I uncovered my unbearable fears. But we laughed a lot, too. I always came home with flushed cheeks and the crazy notion that I could do hard things. I could carry my load that day.

The entire family came to cheer for me at the marathon. They were at mile 1, mile 20 and mile 26.2. The older children held signs, waved orange pom-poms, and shouted out to me. Lily was disinterested and slumped in her stroller. The medication wasn't working. I hugged her and gave her a big kiss. I ran for both of us.

Running down my dream kept me two steps ahead of despair. The unexpected, protracted trial I was facing gave focus and purpose to my marathon dream. My training schedule gave routine, energy, and sustaining friendship to my uncertainty. Achieving what I set out to do reminded me that I can do hard things one step at a time.

Psychologist Howard Gardner outlines eight different types of intelligence in his groundbreaking theory on multiple intelligences (see also Chapter 7). The first two aptitudes, logical-mathematical and linguistic, are the most valued by our society; the others—kinesthetic, interpersonal, musical, naturalist, spatial, and existential intelligence—are less so. When Emily Orton discovered her daughter had Down syndrome, it wasn't her logical-mathematical and linguistic strengths that were her ballast, it was her existential intelligence—the ability to ask and then answer life's big questions.

After the heartbreak of Lily's diagnosis, Emily had a choice: she could give in to fear and sorrow or she could channel her pain into a dream. Training for and running a marathon gave her a refuge, a way to make meaning of her "protracted trial." It also helped Emily discover an ability to do hard things, to run toward her dreams and find hope for her daughter's future. Our challenges can be a blessing if we use them as a springboard for our dreams, pushing us to go places and do things we might not have imagined possible.

Tereza Nemessanyi is another example of dreams emerging from our deepest challenges. While grieving her mother's death, Tereza was inspired to launch Honestly Now (honestlynow.com), a digital platform that provides advice to women struggling with questions both trivial and profound.

Tereza Nemessanyi: *My Honest Moment*

The inspiration to create my startup, Honestly Now, came at a dark moment. My mother had just died, and I stood in front of the mirror, getting dressed to deliver her eulogy. Mom had been my best friend, biggest fan, and she was always the one to tell me the truth when I needed to hear it. Trying on her red blouse, I instinctively turned to ask her, "Is it okay to wear red for a funeral?" In that moment, I realized, I wouldn't ever hear her advice, or feel her warm hug, ever again. My father had recently died as well, and as a new mom myself, I felt deeply alone—like the last one standing, with people who needed me but not sure how I'd step forward.

Realizing that many women lack a support structure when they need it most, I set out to build the beta for Honestly Now—a digital platform to help people get honest feedback from their friends—delivering the advice, affirmation, and warm hug I used to get from my mom. We initially designed Honestly Now to help on questions about our personal appearance—you post a picture, and your friends and experts vote. Am I a vanity case? Maybe, maybe not. But because I saw women frequently confounded with how to present themselves to the world, especially through transitions such as parenting, divorce, health issues, and aging, I wanted to give them confidence by affirming them, and connecting them to people who could help. Just as importantly, though, my MBA-brain could define and describe this market, size it, and engineer a way to turn it into a business. I had a coherent, cohesive business plan. We seeded our beta with my friends, women like me.

As I described the vision of Honestly Now to people, some "got it," but some clearly didn't. A confident group, venture capitalists tend not to be the type to reconsider their decisions once made. One prominent VC had difficulty grasping the concept of "local aesthetic services." Too broad, he said. Pick one vertical and one geography and roll it out that way—such as New Yorkers' hair. This felt much too far away from my moment in front of the mirror. Perhaps the world needed a "hair app"—but I didn't feel I was the one to bring it forth.

In his book on Lean Startups, Eric Ries describes that what people say and what they actually do are often very different things. As we launched Honestly Now, this quickly turned out to be true for us as well. People cared only a little amount about their appearance every day—and then rapidly moved on to a whole host of other thorny life questions.

Tania pitched out a question about thank you notes: is it okay to send your son's thank you notes via cubby mail at school? Marla needed to know—should she use the picture of her scuba diving for her Match.com profile? Going through a divorce, an anonymous asker discovered her husband had a fling with her best friend and neighbor, and their sons are best friends. Should she tell her son about what happened? All important. All real. All very engaging.

So, we pivoted, and decided—ask about any decision you're making, from any dimension of your life. If it's important to you, it's important for us, and we'll find you advice for it.

This broadening of scope in fact nudged us far closer to my seminal moment years earlier. When I'd wanted to ask mom if I looked okay in her blouse, what I really wanted to know was that I wasn't alone. I needed to feel validated and to walk out confident, not second-guessing. Women instinctively float out dilemmas to our friends, for research and affirmation. I wanted to put this instinct in your pocket, so that confidence would be available to you anytime and anywhere.

We relaunched Honestly Now 2.0 and announced a round of funding. There is much more to do, with constant changes afoot based on what we continue to learn. We're incredibly energized by the potential of Honestly Now, and the value— better decisions—our users are already making from it.

Tereza turned one of the most difficult moments of her life into an opportunity to support other women in their struggles, which helped her make meaning of her own. Pursuing a dream can have a therapeutic effect—often we face challenges emerging from forces beyond our control. Dreaming activates us and helps us feel more in control as we make meaningful choices about who we want to become.

TELLING THE STORIES OF OUR LIVES

The stories we absorb as children affect our ideas of whom and what we will be. Perhaps more important are the stories we tell ourselves as adults, as these define our sense of what is possible. Stories help us make meaning of both the bad and the good things that happen in our lives. And stories can give us the courage to dream. Robert Atkinson, PhD, author of *The Gift of Stories*, wrote, "There is a power in storytelling that can transform our lives. Traditional stories, myths, and fairy tales hold this power. The stories we tell of our own lives carry this transforming power, too. In the process of telling our life stories, we discover that we are more sacred beings than we are human beings, that the most powerful life story expresses the struggle of [our] soul."

As a teen, Maria Carr (mariacarr.com) came with her family to the United States as political refugees from Cuba. Maria is a professional actress, wife, and mother. While still in Cuba, Maria's mother Mamina told her children a story that has been pivotal in encouraging Maria's dreams.

Maria Carr: *Nourishing the Soul through Stories*

It was many years after we left Cuba before I wanted to eat split pea soup, even though my mother's split pea soup is delicious.

Cuba is a tropical country where things grow freely, but communist controls greatly limited the food available. Everything had been rationed since Fidel Castro took power, and the grocery stores often had nothing at all. Even if something was allowed on your ration card, you could only buy what they had at the store. My mother stood in line for hours hoping to buy some food, a pair of shoes, anything.

For a VERY long time, *chicharos* (split peas) were the only thing she could buy, but there was no ham or chorizo to flavor the soup.

My mother continued buying and making the *chicharos* because she knew they had a lot of nutritional value. It seemed that we ate *chicharos* for every meal for weeks on end. Mamina used whatever she could from our vegetable patch to flavor them, but often they seemed just a tasteless green mash. My sisters and I grew very tired of split pea soup and dreaded mealtime.

Mamina would set out the three bowls of soup for my sisters, Isis and Nina, and for me. She spoon fed the baby, Nina, and at times when Isis and I complained more than we ate, she would reach over and put a spoonful of soup in our mouths also.

During this time my father was in a labor camp, for the crime of wanting to leave the country, and my mother struggled to care for us, alone and with few provisions. One day she went out to the back patio to do the wash and saw a cute little frog sitting by the door to the kitchen. My mother has always liked frogs, and this frog by the kitchen door gave her an idea. She began to spin wonderful stories about a crazy, adventurous frog named Antonica who would overcome great odds with her daring and creativity. Antonica helped us dream of freedom and possibilities. These exciting tales were reserved for mealtime. We ate until our bowls were empty, distracted from the bland food by the flavor of Antonica's world. Mamina knew her children were well nourished, comforted, and prepared for the challenges and adventures to come.

In 2007, I was preparing to host a TV show on a local station and was struggling with self-doubt. With encouragement and coaching from a friend, I finally realized that I had been preparing for this opportunity most of my life. All I needed was confidence in myself, the kind of confidence Antonica had taught me about, way back in Cuba.

Through this process of self-discovery, the idea came to me to start cooking with my mother. We all loved my Mamina's cooking, but I had never been interested in learning to cook like her. I began to write down her recipes and take pictures of her delicious food. I also started to write down the stories I had heard from my parents, of our lives in Cuba and coming to the United States. At some point I realized I had ninety recipes. This is a significant number to Cuban exiles, as there are ninety miles between Cuba and Key West, Florida. A relatively short distance, but oh, so far!

My effort to grow closer to my mother through cooking became another dream waiting to be fulfilled, through a book called *90 Miles 90 Recipes: My Journey to Understanding*. My mother now seemed as significant as our journey to the United States.

While learning how she orchestrated these flavors, I began to understand my mother as a woman with many gifts. Through cooking together, my appreciation for her has grown. I've come to realize why feeding everyone was so important to her. Nourishing the body is part of nurturing the soul.

My mother is doing very poorly now. Most of my time in the last few months has been dedicated to caring for her. Though our book has not yet been published, it has already proven valuable. It has taught me about dreams from a different perspective—helping me recognize that the lives my sisters and I enjoy are the realization of my parents' dream of freedom and opportunity for them, and especially for us.

Maria's mother's stories have been transformative. The exploits of Antonica the frog were a distraction for Maria during her childhood in Cuba. Decades later, Antonica is a powerful metaphor, one that buoys Maria when she is plagued by self-doubt, reminding her of her parents' sacrifice and legacy. These childhood tales have opened up her imagination to new possibilities, giving her the power to dream.

CRAFTING YOUR PERSONAL NARRATIVE

Psychologist Dan P. McAdams, author of *The Redemptive Self: Stories Americans Live By*, writes: "[Our personal] narratives guide behavior in every moment, and frame not only how we see the past but how we see ourselves in the future."

Our stories often predict our future, even as we make meaning of the past. Emily Orton's story foretells that she will again do hard things, and Maria Carr's that she will confidently face future struggles. Macy Robison (macyrobison.com), a vocalist and music educator, has made meaning of her life experiences through the creation of a cabaret-style recital titled *Children Will Listen: Reflections on Mothering*.

Macy Robison: *Making Meaning through Music*

As a singer, my favorite songs to perform are those that tell a story. To sing for vocal beauty's sake is not interesting to me—I'm a sucker for a good story. My love of story initially drew me to perform in a cabaret-style production of a musical. That experience gave me the longing to jump into the local cabaret scene in Boston, but I couldn't get myself started. I think I secretly believed no one really needed to hear my voice or story—there were so many others singing and doing a better job than I could have done.

Through Whitney's encouragement, I finally became motivated to create my own cabaret show and talk about something

I really cared about—being a mother. I was a new mom, and was so thrilled to be living this dream, for which I had waited a very long time. I learned songs and prepared the cabaret, but it wasn't clicking. As I continued to refine the material, one day it occurred to me that the story I wanted to tell and needed to tell was my journey as a woman and a mother. Again, I doubted. I believed that no one really wanted to hear what a mother with an eight-month-old wanted to say. The women I would be performing for were far more seasoned and wise in their mothering. But telling my own story felt right. So I began. And as I did, the lyrics in the songs written by someone else for another show became my lyrics and my story.

The story of my preparation to become a mother (including the grief at the loss of my own mother at a young age) has helped me catch a vision of the mother and the woman I want to be. Our stories need to be told. Our stories help us connect. And we can tell them using the medium that is the most comfortable for us. For me, it was singing. For someone else, it could be blogging or quilting or building a career or raising a child. The most important thing is that we tell the story.

Macy has found joy and fulfillment in sharing her story through music. She has crafted a personal narrative about her journey to motherhood, and her story is now inspiring others to examine their lives, loves, and dreams. Listening to someone else's story often helps us view our own dreams through a different lens. We also process our sorrows and our losses, and find hope in telling our own stories. Dreaming is essential to making meaning of our lives—dreaming lifts us out of what has happened in what is often a confusing, messy, and painful past so that we can craft a narrative that predicts a brighter future. And often, as we dream, we better understand the significance of our lives, what they are now and what they can become.

FRAMING YOUR PAST, PREDICTING YOUR FUTURE...

Don't be satisfied with stories of how things have gone with others. Unfold your own myth.
—Rumi, thirteenth-century Persian poet

- What are the personal narratives that frame your past, and possibly predict the future and achievement of your dreams?
- What are the sorrows in your life? Can you build dreams that help make sense of your sadness?
- How can telling stories help us discover or rediscover our dreams? What cues can we find about our dreams in the stories we most often tell (and those we don't) about our lives?
- How do the stories we tell ourselves when we're alone differ from those we tell our family and friends, our children, or those whom we mentor? For example, stories that I tell my children and mentees tend to be well crafted and confident. Stories I share with my peers are less-polished recountings of personal experiences, both happy and sad. The stories I tell myself are rarely as upbeat.
- Consider the words of writer and theologian Frederick Buechner: "God calls you to the place where your deep gladness and the world's deep hunger meet." If you were to craft a narrative using that quote as a starting point, what story would you tell, whether written, painted, danced, photographed, or sung?

2

TO FIND YOUR VOICE,
TO FIND YOURSELF

When I went on sabbatical from my job on Wall Street, I started taking voice lessons. This was a big risk for me. *Really* big. Yes, I majored in music, but my emphasis was piano. I was good at accompanying vocalists as they sang classical, Broadway, and religious music, but removing myself from the bulwark of the piano and attempting to actually sing was terrifying.

Even though I could generally sing on pitch, my vocal talent was nowhere near my keyboard expertise. My voice teacher kindly, pithily, and accurately described my voice when she quipped, "I'm sure there's vibrato in there somewhere. We'll just have to find it."

As my life got busy again, I stopped taking lessons. I remain wistful about learning to sing. Perhaps I'll try again someday. I do wonder: Why do I want to sing *so* much? Why am I hooked on reality shows that involve singing? Perhaps it's because singing is about finding my voice, especially my figurative voice, the one that declares, "This is who I am," "This is what I have to say... do... share."

DISCOVERING YOUR UNIQUE VOICE

In *Writing to Change the World,* author Mary Pipher declares: "Voice is everything we are, all that we have observed, the emotional chords that are uniquely ours—all our flaws and all of our strengths, expressed in words that best reflect us. Voice is like a snowflake—complicated, beautiful, and individual. It is essence of self, distilled and offered in service to the world...."

Chrysula Winegar (chrysulawinegar.com), originally from Australia, is a work-at-home mother with nearly two decades' experience at blue-chip corporations. Currently authoring her first book *When You Wake Up a Mother,* Chrysula describes below what it was like to lose her voice, and then to gradually rediscover this essence of her self.

Chrysula Winegar: *"Oh My Goodness. I Left My Voice on the Bus."*

I wanted to stay home full-time with my children. My mother sometimes wasn't able to, and she sometimes didn't want to: both are reasons I respect. My husband and I discussed the decision at length. He was home for a time with our eldest two children while growing his business; I took on the role of primary breadwinner. For some families it works. It didn't for us.

Most days, being at home is enough. I have amazing children. I was never this smart at their ages, never this spiritually connected, certainly never this interesting. I love being my children's mother. However, after a few years of being at home full-time, I realized something was missing. I did not feel heard.

Partnering with my husband for eight years in his private art consultancy, and now running that business fully on my own, has helped me feel heard. I love beautiful things and I love sharing them with people. Art has the capacity to speak without language, to fill voids of which we're not even aware. I am privileged to have access to so much visual conversation. But it's behavior, people, words that make me feel alive, make me feel that I haven't somehow left my voice, disembodied, on a bus aimlessly trolling the streets of New York.

A few years ago I had a letter to the editor published in *The New York Times*. It was an incredible moment. In just a few sentences, I was able to express things that had been on my mind for more than a year. The act of publishing connected me to thousands of people who were thinking the same thoughts and, even better, to thousands more to whom those thoughts hadn't occurred. It felt as if I had begun a conversation with New York.

Since my early twenties, I've been intrigued by the relationship between organizations and families. A consultancy business and a PhD thesis are both being constructed in my mind. I recently realized that I don't need the full-fledged second business and the prefix Dr. just yet. What I need is to be part of the conversation. What I hunger for is to participate, even at the fringes, in the topics I feel passionate about.

I started a blog titled *Work. Life. Balance.* Writing allows me to give free rein to thoughts that have been bubbling away for years. On Twitter I can participate by sound bite and get access to all the data and discussion I need. I can read/listen as much or as little as my other responsibilities allow. These tools provide a sense of engagement, of participation, of dialogue—especially when both friends and strangers give back through their often profound and intimate comments. I'm part of a rich conversation. I'm listening, plugged in to the research, the debate, the buzz. And I have things to say. Oh boy, do I ever.

In the meantime, my two eldest children are becoming more interesting. They are becoming aware of other people, and their thoughts are beginning to develop. As they expand their capacity for social interaction, I'm able to engage with them on richer levels. We all benefit. I loved them as babies and toddlers and preschoolers. When we aren't fighting, I truly adore them as they learn and grow through these next stages. As I have listened and tried to understand their emerging voices, their attempts to listen back enable my own voice. The first inklings of their wanting to understand me are a gift, a recognition that we're beginning to develop real two-way relationships.

In the convergence of reading, writing, speaking, listening, I'm finding a flow of authenticity and personal truth. My family life and professional interests are merging. As they integrate, I feel heard. I have my voice back.

I especially like this from Chrysula: "As I listen and try to understand [my children's] emerging voices, their attempts to listen back enable my own voice." True conversation—the sharing of ideas and the feeling of being heard, something that for many (me included) is happening via social media platforms—further enables us to find our voices, as well as to discover our dreams.

STRENGTHENING YOUR VOICE
THROUGH CHALLENGES

Finding your voice often comes through facing challenges. In the book *The Maiden King,* Robert Bly and Marion Woodman observe, "For thousands of years, a powerful voice was a mark of personhood. The longer the person stayed in the underworld (plunged to the depths of sorrow, for example) the more powerful the voice." There are myriad examples of women who, after years of sorrow, loss, or other challenges, have emerged as powerful voices for change in the world.

LaNola Kathleen Stone (lanola.com), an artist, photographer, and the author of *Photographing Childhood: The Image and the Memory,* shares her experience of falling into and climbing back out of the abyss of sorrow.

LaNola Kathleen Stone: *Rebirth of the Creative Self*

Since I was very young, I've had an active creative pull. In my teen years, the tools of photography allowed me to express and share my creative meanderings in images. Over the past two decades, I have invested time and resources to develop this gift through my university education, a move to New York City, and subsequent graduate school.

Now, not all of the images I shot were drawn from organic intuition. The photographs that I labeled my personal work, and which I deemed as having little commercial value, were often pushed aside so I could continue to develop my professional portfolio and make a living as a shooter. I knew that my personal work fed my creative spirit, but the roar of a hungry tummy was more audible. I took the images and ideas that played in my creative mind for granted, utilizing them once in a while but never gifting them the way they gifted me. And, when I turned my attention to maintaining a marriage with a verbally abusive man, the vibrant images began to fade and were eventually gone.

It was a tangible absence and the hole left was deep. I had never known life without ideas and images and I was worried that they'd never return.

We all know when our life is out of balance; it just doesn't feel right. I liken this to a "perfect" shirt that is too tight, or a beautiful shoe that has heels that are too high. I knew the balance in my life was gone, but I worked very hard to stand up straight in those heels that were too high and suck in my gut for that shirt that was too small. If I could only conform to another's expectations and make my marriage work, then the balance would return, right? But in a marriage, the balance of each is achieved by the efforts of both. So no matter how hard I tried, I alone could not make our marriage work. He pursued his goals without respect for me, but the rage and frustration around his career and life were increasingly directed toward me. His rants grew longer and, although my husband never hit me, his grabbing and shaking increased. I knew it was not right, but the tirades and horrible name-calling, grabbing, and shaking became normal. I adjusted, but a part of me had to die to make room for this new normal.

When his decisions eventually led to our divorce, my time was then filled with the heavy silence of being alone, alone without a husband and without the gift of the images that had once creatively danced in my imagination before the abuse. The silence was deafening.

I was sad as long as I needed to be sad, and upset as long as it took, but the journey from that low to being truly happy and fulfilled today (just two and a half years later) came through validating creative promptings, something I'd done little of while distracted by my situation of abuse. I mourned the loss of one life, but as I surrounded myself with positive and creative ideas, I began to investigate the possibilities of another. Like our gifts and our talents, ultimately, our pasts come in various shapes and sizes and it's what we do with our past that defines us, not merely the past itself.

Six months after my divorce, the images finally began to appear again. Now I validate them, all of them. Through my validation, I have completed graduate school, won scholarships and awards, am currently working on a book deal, had my work shown during one of the most prestigious art fairs in the United States, Art Basel Miami, and have been able to teach and mentor young undergraduate photographers. These results have both surprised and delighted me.

I now acknowledge my gift, and it never fails to give back. These images are my white rabbit beckoning me to awaiting adventures. I don't always know what is down the rabbit hole, or where it will take me, but I do know that to trust my inner self is paramount. In this my creative self has been reborn and is thriving. In this is my happiness.

USING YOUR WORDS

As we face our own challenges, we must remember that we have a voice, and having a voice is powerful. We all have something to say, but many of us simply need to learn how to speak, whether through words written or spoken, images, music, movement— whatever medium enables our voice. We admonish young children to "Use your words!" especially as an alternative to screaming or hitting a sibling when they don't get what they want. As children, we don't always know how to express our emotions, and as women we often experience the same problem, even though we are adults. Our emotions overwhelm us and we don't know how to express our most deeply held views. We don't have the words, or we haven't had a rational moment to craft what we most want to say, but there is great power in "using our words."

When the Berlin Wall came down in 1989, the world rejoiced. In celebrating the twentieth anniversary of its fall, I reflected on the kind of conviction, the kind of voice, required to break down walls—be they miles of concrete in a former Communist region or invisible but no-less-apparent barricades in an office setting, or in our community or home.

Would the Berlin Wall have fallen without President Reagan's 1987 speech challenging Mikhail Gorbachev to "tear down this wall"? Probably, but not as quickly. Yet according to *The Wall Street Journal*, officials in the State Department, the National Security Council, and the White House all pushed Reagan to deep-six his "tear down this wall" rhetoric. They warned that Reagan's "sock-it-to-'em" line would incense Gorbachev and fray relations. Reagan left the line in. The wall came tumbling down.

SPEAKING OUT WITH CONVICTION

As a sell-side analyst on Wall Street, the stakes were obviously much lower for me than they were for Reagan. Money was involved, but not lives or freedom. I nonetheless struggled to be decisive in assigning a buy or sell rating to a stock. When I upgraded, short investors were unhappy. If I downgraded a stock, the reactions were even worse; not only were long investors unhappy, the executives and owners whose net worth stood to dwindle were steamed.

I eventually learned what President Reagan knew. The only safe harbor is our convictions. Safe not because it proves we are right, or guarantees our popularity, but safe because it ensures we are honest to our core values. Articulating our beliefs tears down walls of our own insecurities and clears the way for others to change.

Although speaking from conviction might require us to say something others don't want to hear, it's not unkind. Gorbachev might not have wanted to hear, "Mr. Gorbachev, tear down this wall," but President Reagan wasn't throwing him under the bus. On the contrary, he was saying, "Mr. Gorbachev, you have the opportunity to do something grand and good. It will require sacrifice, but I believe you're up to the challenge."

Learning to make a decisive stock call was terribly difficult. I didn't want people to be mad at me. However, it got easier when I had a boss who encouraged, even challenged me—"*You aren't a shrinking violet!*"—to be decisive, to have an opinion. His belief that I could do something grand within my sphere of stock picking was a turning point. Perhaps President Reagan's words were a turning point for Mr. Gorbachev as well.

I believe the same is true for you and me.

Reagan's speechwriters discouraged him. His challenge would be unpopular. In my own situation, I feared antagonizing those with whom I worked. And yet, just as the world needed to hear what Reagan had to say, the world needs to hear what you and I have to say. Our point of view, our feminine point of view, matters. It matters to encourage others and advocate for the grand and good things that are our dreams. In fact, I believe one of the most important things I learned while working in the financial sector was to "use my words."

Buddhist monk Maha Ghosananda was quoted by author Jacqueline Novogratz in *The Blue Sweater:* "If you move through the world only with your intellect, then you walk on only one leg. If you move through the world only with your compassion, then you walk on only one leg. But if you move through the world with both intellect and compassion, then you have wisdom."

Elizabeth Harmer Dionne, a retired attorney who is currently pursuing her PhD in political science at Boston College, is a woman who is using her words to defend one of her dreams, that of being a mother.

Elizabeth Harmer Dionne: *The Economics of Motherhood*

Children are expensive. The projected lifetime cost for raising a child range from $180,000 to $290,000 to well north of
one million dollars, depending on the neighborhood, posses-
sions, and education a family selects.

Raising children exacts other costs. One study reported that
93 percent of "highly qualified" women who wanted to reenter the workforce after raising children were unable to return to
their chosen career. In other words, there's a robust off-ramp
and an anemic on-ramp. Another study found that professional
women who have a child experience a 10 to 15 percent drop in
subsequent earnings. Numerous studies indicate that professional women still bear a disproportionate share of childrear-
ing and housekeeping duties.

Linda Hirshman's controversial book *Get to Work: A Manifesto
for Women of the World* verbally lashed highly educated women
who opt out of the workforce in order to raise their children.
According to Hirshman, such women fail the collective good of
all women by succumbing to the pressures of a sexist culture.
They perpetuate unequal pay and professional glass ceilings.

A recent issue of *Wellesley* magazine highlighted alumnae
who chose to stay home. One woman stated that the hours
she put into parenting made her a better mother than one
who worked. The professional women who wrote letters to the
editor were livid. However, there is an undeniable logic to the
alumna's statement. Doing something part-time (including
parenting) does not render one a failure, or even merely inad-
equate. Nonetheless, there is a certain proficiency that follows
effort and experience. There are variations in inherent ability,
but performance typically improves with practice.

I left the practice of law when it became clear that my autistic son needed an advocate. The collective chaos of managing three children, a fourth pregnancy, two nannies, a housekeeper, and a demanding career finally overwhelmed me. My husband and I considered hiring someone to manage our autistic son's education and therapies, but I simply couldn't delegate his care. I needed firsthand knowledge of his diagnosis and how to treat it.

Leaving professional life was hard. I walked away from friends, a schedule, a salary, and social stature. I plunged into full-time parenting, something at which I was not proficient—something that still perplexes me! However, remaining in the workforce would have been harder. I made a free choice, fully apprised of the risk I took, and I have never looked back.

Philosopher Ayn Rand believed there is no such thing as sacrifice. Rather, there are only rational decisions that bring us closer to our ultimate goals. In other words, the choices we make are irrefutable evidence of what we value. Even generous acts reflect a set of values. Living in accordance with those values gratifies us, hence our gain outweighs our loss.

In a world of scarcity and competing demands, Rand's view has a certain hard-nosed rationality. We give up something we want for something we want more. We each have a single life, made up of finite seconds that tick inexorably away. How we choose to spend each day both expresses our values and carries us closer to our ultimate goals, even if we have never articulated precisely what those values and goals are.

I was fortunate that my decision to come home had a positive, even miraculous, outcome for my son. Others make similar decisions without such obvious payback. I still have professional aspirations, and I'm pursuing them wholeheartedly, but I will not return to the practice of law. My time at home focused my values and helped me understand what I want to do with my remaining days, months, and years.

Criticizing highly educated women who "opt out" ignores two realities: the first is that society reaps tremendous, tangible benefits from able women (and men) who have the time to cultivate their families, neighborhoods, schools, churches, and politics. If all the capable people are working eighty hours a week, who will tend to our children, communities, and culture? Second, some values are intangible. Not everything can be monetized. It is good, and even necessary, that women be represented in all walks of professional life, because it expands the world of possibility for all women. However, there are values that defy commodification, such as the well-being of our children and even ourselves. There is also the opportunity to perpetuate our values through generations to come. By raising children well, we leave an indelible mark on posterity. Surely this is a rational choice that is worth the cost.

In learning to use our words, we believe what we say matters, that our opinions are as important as our encouraging words. What we think and say can summon the best in others; it can also be an important tool for achieving our dreams. For instance, were someone to question Elizabeth's decision to leave the workforce, I'm confident that she would have at least five well-crafted talking points that articulate her reasons. We can have our talking points too. Said Natalie Goldberg, author of *Writing Down the Bones*, "Once you have learned to trust your own voice...you have the basic tool to fulfill your dreams."

ACTIVATING YOUR NAME

An important piece of finding your voice is activating your name. In his book *The Checklist Manifesto*, Atul Gawande explains that complicated processes like surgery, where human error can lead to tragedy, require checklists. One of the most important, but often seen as superfluous, steps in his Surgical Safety Checklist is to make sure everyone in the operating room knows each other by name. Gawande found that when introductions were made before surgery, the average number of complications and deaths fell by 35 percent. He attributed this dip to the "activation phenomenon": having gotten a chance to voice their names, people were much more likely to speak up later if they saw a problem.

On a recent visit to a university campus, I experienced the emboldening power of names firsthand. After announcing my last name to the parking lot sentry, whom I hadn't seen for months, he asked, "Is your first name Whitney?" A number of luminaries pass in and out of that parking lot daily, yet this man remembered my name; I found myself sitting a little taller. Taking the positive influence of names even further, many have credited Bill Clinton's remarkable political success to his prowess at not only reading people but also remembering their names.

Just as hearing or saying your name can boost your confidence, not hearing your name can detract from it. For example, as I was writing this chapter, my colleagues and I cohosted a business event. When introductions were made, my name was inadvertently omitted. All were aware of the omission as soon as it happened, but it was done. When I thought to chime in during the question-and-answer session (and ordinarily would have), I couldn't quite. Because I had not been named, self-doubt crept in, and I found myself unable to fully participate.

Any words that people use to name us or, more generally speaking, to label us deeply affect our identity. *The Zookeeper's Wife* is the story of Jan and Antonina Zabinski, Polish Christian zookeepers who, horrified by Nazi racism, managed to save more than three hundred people. Author Diane Ackerman writes movingly about Polish émigré Eva Hoffman's psychic earthquake of having to shed her name in order to save her life: "Nothing much has happened, except a small, seismic mental shift. The twist in our names takes them a tiny distance from us—but it is a gap into which the infinite hobgoblin of abstraction enters."

Suddenly Eva Hoffman's given name, and that of her sister, no longer exists even though "they were as surely us as our eyes or hands." The new names were actually "identification tags, disembodied signs pointing to objects that happen to be my sister and myself. We walk to our seats, into a roomful of unknown faces, with names that make us strangers to ourselves."

DISCOVERING WHO YOU ARE

Our names, our identities, our figuring out "This is who I am" are a huge part of discovering our dreams. And haven't many of us said, "I'll start dreaming once I wrap up with X, Y, or Z project." At the same time, we are asking ourselves, "Why do I keep putting things off? There's so much to do but I can't get anything done."

Perhaps we have it backwards. Perhaps having goals for ourselves is not something to do after we've wrapped up X, Y, and Z projects. Perhaps daring to dream is a goal we need to pursue now, because it's key to getting those X, Y, and Z projects done.

Psychologist Timothy Pychyl writes in an article titled "Teenagers, Identity Crises, and Procrastination" that if we can't answer the questions "Who am I?" and "What am I?" we're more likely to procrastinate. In other words, the more people know who they are, the less likely they are to procrastinate. Pychyl explains the interconnectedness between identity and agency as follows: "Identity is that knowledge of who we are.... Agency is the belief that we are in control of our decisions and responsible for our outcomes.... It means we make a difference, we make things happen, we act on the world. Thus, being an active agent depends on identity, or knowing who we are."

Perhaps, then, the best thing we can do is to put our busyness to the side, and instead focus on our identity and our dreams—or, as management consultant Robin Dickinson said after he read Pychyl's study, "Focus on your *To-Be List*, before the *To-Do List*." When we return to that to-do list we might just find we're actually beginning to get things done.

Through dreaming, we can find our voice and know who we are. When we have a clear sense of identity, we can make things happen and act on the world; we can then speak the words that make our dreams become a reality.

USING YOUR WORDS...

The human voice is the most beautiful instrument of all, but it is the most difficult to play.
　　　　　　　—Richard Strauss, nineteenth-century composer

- What if you had words to describe your dreams and to advocate for your dreams and the people you love? Would being able to articulate your thoughts—verbally or in writing—help your dreams come true?
- If you speak a foreign language, are you bolder in that second tongue? Do you say what you mean in a way that you don't in your native tongue? As you are learning

to advocate for your dreams, how can you draw on that "second tongue" confidence?

- Does participating in social networking and regularly sharing your point of view—such as by blogging or tweeting—help you find your words and feel your way toward your dream?

- We may know what our children want, but we ask them to use their words. Why is this important for them? Why is it important for us?

- What can you do today to find your own voice, to trust that voice, to acquire the tools needed to achieve your dream? Can you try saying out loud, kindly, civilly what you really want, or really think, to your children, husband, friends, coworkers?

- How is learning to say your name—to value it, to know that it means something—key to your dreaming?

- If you're feeling you want to get more done, what would happen if you focused on your identity for even a few moments a day?

3

TO TRULY GROW UP

Not long ago, as part of a "go for your life goals" pep rally, I spoke to a group of young women ranging in age from thirteen to seventeen. As I prepared to rally the girls, I couldn't help but recall my early days on Wall Street.

I had just started working as a sales assistant at Smith Barney. Near my desk was the *bullpen*, which is what we called the spot where newly recruited stockbrokers (mostly men) sat. Their job involved cold calling potential clients in order to open new accounts and sell stocks. Because testosterone ran high in this locker room of twenty-something men, and there was intense pressure to meet their quotas, they inevitably went for the hard sell.

"It doesn't take a rocket scientist to know that buying this stock makes sense," they would say. To waffling male prospects they'd taunt, "Throw down your pom-poms and get in the game."

I liked the first expression but I took offense at the latter one. I had been a cheerleader in high school. I had *aspired* to be a cheerleader, and I loved cheerleading. It was an important part of my identity in high school. Here were these guys, essentially equating cheerleading with being a wimp. The older I get, however, the more I find myself wanting to say, not to men, but to women, "Throw down your pom-poms and get in the game!"

Perhaps that's why the story of Judy Dushku, an associate professor of government at Suffolk University in Boston, resonated so strongly with me. A mother of four, stepmother of four, grandmother of eight, great-grandmother of one, and founder of THARCE-Gulu, Inc. (tharce-gulu.org), Judy is definitely in the game.

Judith Dushku: *Have I Done Any Good?*

My best ideas, or dreams, are narrated by hymns my mother sang to me as a child, whether she wanted to make a point, or exhort me to some noble act, or upbraid me. One of her favorites, which she would punctuate with her pointed teaching finger, began with the words:

Have I done any good in the world today?
Have I helped anyone in need?

Perhaps, therefore, it was inevitable that I would launch a nongovernmental organization (NGO) known as THARCE-Gulu, Inc., (Trauma Healing and Reflection Center) in northern Uganda for victims of war.

I have taught comparative politics for forty-five years, and teaching African politics has been a favorite endeavor. In recent years, I have been compelled to focus on the discouraging fact that Africa has been too often a place of proxy-wars over strategic location and power, and wars over who will control and profit from the continent's vast resources. I've been driven to explore and try to understand how the populations of war-ravaged places recover, how individuals forced to fight these wars return to productive lives.

From 2001 to 2003, while serving as dean of a small satellite campus my university maintains in Dakar, Senegal, I became close to refugees from wars in Sierra Leone and Liberia. I learned of the commonplace practice of abducting children to fight vicious wars and commit unthinkable acts under threats of death or torture, as well as the taking by competing war lords of girl-children into captivity. Some girls spent years in the bush with rebel leaders who beat, raped, and impregnated them, used them as cooks and carriers of supplies, and then killed them; some ultimately escaped, often struggling to protect their children. If they did find "home," they were often stigmatized for having been "child soldiers."

In 2008, I met Lina Zedriga, an international lawyer and activist in Uganda who worked supporting former abductees, especially child mothers, who sought to restore their lives to productivity. Shortly thereafter I took a student trip to Kampala to study Ugandan politics. Lina brought former child soldiers she was mentoring from Gulu to meet us. After hearing their shocking stories, I determined that I had to do something to help these children.

In July 2010, I took a group of thirteen women from throughout the United States, Canada, and Mexico to build homes in a community in Gulu, Uganda, alongside former abductees. These homes are for those who have lost children to the war, and who now care for war orphans. We were there to offer serious help, to "get our hands dirty" placing bricks in clay-mud and preparing the bamboo strips for rope to hold down the grass roofs. We also held babies, sang with little children, and bought cloth bags and clothes sewn by village women. We admired their work, laughed and danced with them, and we cried when they told us of their years in the bush and what they had endured, or of waiting at home for children stolen from their lives.

Psychologists in Gulu who specialize in trauma said that this sharing of stories with respectful listeners was one very helpful method used for trauma healing. We hoped our listening with compassion, as we worked with them shoulder to shoulder, would contribute to that process in some small way.

Have I cheered up the sad, or made someone feel glad? If not I have failed indeed.

On breaks from laying bricks, we were shown the gardens where women grew vegetables and a school that had recently been finished for the youngest children living there. The community is incredibly poor, but some are moving beyond their pasts and embracing life anew. We felt part of their complex journey to recovery.

I don't know what THARCE-Gulu, Inc., will do next. A few women from this trip hope to organize home-building trips of their own. Plans for a workshop on art therapy emerged, where Ugandans from Gulu and Americans will work together at Lina's Center. Some want to help build a bakery with child-mothers who seek to establish new businesses in Gulu. And filmmaking plans abound.

I was ill with food poisoning the night we left Uganda for home, and for two days I was sick and restless in bed. But a sense of peace broke through when the words of my mother's hymn flooded my mind:

Has anyone's burden been lighter today because I was willing to share? Have the sick and the weary been helped on their way? When they needed my help was I there?

CLAIMING A CENTRAL PLACE IN YOUR STORY

What Judy is accomplishing is no easy task. In fact, it's note-worthy that she is in her sixties because learning to both throw down our pom-poms and get in the game can require a lifetime of trial and error. In a *Harvard Business Review* article titled "Do Women Lack Ambition?" Anna Fels, a psychiatrist at Cornell

University, observes that when the dozens of successful women she interviewed told their own stories, "they refused to claim a central, purposeful place."

Were Dr. Fels to interview you, how would you tell your story? Are you using language that suggests you're the supporting actress in your own life? For instance, when someone offers words of appreciation about a dinner you've prepared, a class you've taught, or an event you organized and brilliantly executed, do you gracefully reply "Thank you" or do you say, "It was nothing"?

As Fels tried to understand why women refuse to be the heroes of their own stories, she encountered the Bem Sex-Role Inventory, which confirms that society considers a woman to be feminine only within the context of a relationship and when she is giving something to someone. It's no wonder that a "feminine" woman finds it difficult to get in the game and demand support to pursue her goals. It also explains why she feels selfish when she doesn't subordinate her needs to others.

A successful female CEO recently needed my help. It was mostly business-related but also partly for her. As she started to ask for my assistance, I sensed how difficult it was for her. Advocate on her organization's behalf? Piece of cake. That's one of the reasons her business has been successful. But advocate on her own behalf?

I'll confess that even among my closest friends I find it painful to say, "Look what I did," and so I don't do it very often. If you want to see just how masterful most women have become at deflecting, the next time you're with a group of girlfriends, ask them about something they (not their husband or children) have done well in the past year. Chances are good that each woman will quickly and deftly redirect the conversation far, far away from herself.

"A key type of discrimination that women face is the expectation that feminine women will forfeit opportunities for recognition," says Fels. "When women do speak as much as men in a work situation or compete for high-visibility positions, their femininity is assailed."

My point here isn't to say that relatedness and nurturing and picking up our pom-poms to cheer others on is unimportant. Those qualities are often innate to women. If we set these "feminine" qualities aside or neglect them, we will have lost an irreplaceable piece of ourselves. But to truly grow up, we must learn to throw down our pom-poms, believing we can act and that what we have to offer is a valuable part of who we are. When we recognize this, we give ourselves permission to dream and to encourage the girls and women around us to do the same.

LEARNING FROM THE STORY OF PSYCHE

As we seek to claim a central place in our own stories, we can learn from the myth of Psyche. It is one of the few stories, according to Jungian psychologists Jean Shinoda Bolen and Robert Johnson, that focuses on the psychology of feminine, rather than masculine, development. It is a story that has had a profound impact on me.

Psyche is a mortal woman who wants to find her estranged husband, Eros, god of love and son of Aphrodite. Aphrodite, whose jealous fit led to their meeting and falling in love in the first place, holds the key to their being reunited (it often happens that whatever has wounded us is instrumental in our healing).

Aphrodite assigns Psyche four tasks, all of which are symbolic of skills she needs to develop. Because each task requires her to do more than she feels capable of, Psyche is initially paralyzed by fear. However, because this is the only course that can reunite her with Eros, she chooses to proceed.

Task 1: Sort Seeds (Prioritize)

For the first task, Psyche must sort a huge jumble of corn, barley, and poppy seeds into separate piles before morning. The task seems impossible given her time frame, until an army of ants comes to her aid and helps her sort the seeds.

Sifting through possibilities and establishing personal priorities in the face of conflicting feelings and competing loyalties requires a sorting of the seeds. Sometimes we need to sleep on the problem, letting the industrious collective of ants—our subconscious—work things out. As we learn to trust our intuition, clarity will emerge. Christine Vick, a stay-at-home mom, tells how her dreams emerged as she learned to prioritize.

Christine Vick: *Simply Living*

My college self would be disappointed with my life today.

Back then, I had it all mapped out: graduate in three years with a BA in English (check). Do volunteer work for a few years (check). Get an MA in English Literature (check).

But then I started to go off course: Get a PhD (ummm...). Secure a tenure track position by the time I'm twenty-eight (ummm...again). Have three kids (oops, four) and a white picket fence (nope).

Turns out my eighteen-year-old self couldn't see the whole picture. She couldn't see that I'd be burned out by academia after my master's degree and feel miserable about applying for PhD programs. Or that I'd quite like what I imagined then would be very mundane tasks: cooking, decorating, organizing, and hanging out with my kids. I rarely say this out loud, but I don't even mind cleaning (except for doing the laundry, which is my Achilles heel).

When I was younger, I dismissed any field or career that was less than rigorously academic as "fluff." I don't know where I got this idea, because my parents have encouraged all my efforts and never pushed me in any direction. Nevertheless, this philosophy guided my early decisions and left me feeling like a failure when I found my studies unfulfilling.

By the second year of my MA program, I was unhappy, frustrated, and fed up, but I couldn't admit (even to myself) that I wanted to quit. The dream of being a professor had always defined me, and letting it go made me panic. What would I do? How could my life be relevant?

Pride played a big role, too. I'd always been so vocal about my goals (I'm still learning the value of saying less, a lot less) that I was just plain embarrassed not to follow through, especially when my fellow students were busy being accepted into PhD programs across the country.

My pain eased a bit when I moved East and took a part-time job with a small community newspaper. I was no longer surrounded by academics and it became clear that most people aren't concerned with the roles of Renaissance women, applying continental philosophy to modern texts, or deconstructing old English manuscripts. They're just trying to earn a living, balance hectic lives, and find a little free time.

Two years ago I was approached by a friend of a friend who was starting her own magazine about organizing (a favorite topic and hobby of mine). She was looking for part-time editors and wondered if I'd be interested.

I said yes immediately.

One of the highlights of the job was a trip to North Carolina to interview the Flylady, Marla Cilley. It was my first business trip, albeit with my six-month-old in tow. I enjoyed meeting Cilley, who was fun, vivacious, and full of empathy; hanging out with my boss; eating out; overcoming my fear of prop planes;

and seeing the Biltmore Estate in Asheville. It actually seemed more like a vacation than work, since I normally spend my days in Cinderella mode: scrubbing, cooking, chauffeuring, and trying to be patient with lots of little people with lots of needs.

Being a part of *Organize* magazine not only gave me the experience to start my own website, Store and Style, it taught me a valuable lesson: for a task to be valuable, it doesn't have to be weighty, solemn, or make history.

It just has to be important to me. If it's fun, too, even better.

I love editing—knowing what to add, move around, or rework so an article shines. I love organizing—helping people see how a little order can make life easier and more enjoyable. And I love making school lunches, reading to my son on the front porch while waiting for the bus, baking cookies, and painting my daughter's fingernails. Lucky for me, my life can encompass all of these activities.

Looking back, I'm glad I didn't pressure myself into starting a PhD program—I know I would have quit.

I'm also glad my college self is no longer in charge.

Task 2: Acquire the Golden Fleece (Harness Power)

Aphrodite next orders Psyche to obtain golden fleece from the rams of the sun, huge aggressive beasts in a field, butting heads. This task also seems impossible, for if Psyche goes among the rams, she'll be trampled. This time, instead of ants coming to her aid, the reeds on the river's edge call to her, advising her to wait until sundown when the rams disperse so she can safely pick strands of fleece off the brambles the rams have brushed against. Psyche's ability to acquire the golden fleece without being crushed is a metaphor for every woman's task of gaining power without losing her innate sense of connectedness and compassion.

Task 3: Fill the Crystal Flask (Achieve Goals)

For the third task, Psyche must fill a flask with water from an inhospitable stream, etched into a jagged cliff and guarded by dragons. To help her in this seemingly impossible task, Psyche has help from the eagle of Zeus. The eagle has the ability to see what it wants, plunge from the sky, and grab it with its talons.

Psyche's completion of this task is symbolic of her learning how to set a goal, avoid the pitfalls that will inevitably come (success at this may include delegation), and then achieve her goal. As Jaime Cobb Dubeia mother of one living in New York City, went through a huge career change, she came to terms with achieving her goals—an important aspect of growing up.

Jaime Cobb Dubei: *School's in Session*

Be the change you wish to see in the world.
        —Mahatma Gandhi, twentieth-century political leader

While unhappily working in the heart of the children's clothing industry, I saw ads on the subway that drew me into teaching with the New York City Teaching Fellows (NYCTF). As I embarked on the journey to teach, I thought back to my idealistic days in college, where I knew I wanted to change the world one person at a time. I wanted to make a difference more than I could ever explain. I felt it in the depths of my soul.

I went from working on Thirty-Third Street, in the heart of Herald Square, to the depths of Morrisania in the South Bronx, teaching at one of the most notorious middle schools in New York City. They always say the first year of teaching is rough. September 11th happened four days into my teaching career, leaving me to explain to seventh and eighth graders why two buildings fell. On November 12, 2001, one of my student's parents died in an airplane crash in Belle Harbor, New York. For reasons still unknown, the principal was removed in January 2002. Many days went by where I had no idea who my boss was, what the agenda would be, or how we were accomplishing it.

I kept working, collaborating with my mentor teachers and pursuing my Masters degree and certification. Whatever the children needed, I did my best to provide. When I realized they had no idea what basic geographic features looked like, I found calendars to rip apart and post around the room. I placed a picture of child from Afghanistan in the front, just above the center of the chalkboard. In the middle of a lesson on the U.S. Civil War, Jason raised his hand. I must admit I probably showed my shock, as Jason rarely paid attention and never asked questions.

"Miss, is that really what a girl in Afghanistan looks like?"

"Yes, Jason."

"Wow. I had no idea. She looks just like my cousin."

Five years later, I sat on a hundred-acre farm sixteen miles from the nearest town in Pennsylvania. I was on childcare leave, nursing my nine-month-old daughter while my husband worked at a local college. After dinner one night, I looked up from my laptop and said, "Honey, what if I started a school?"

He immediately said, "Go for it! What kind are you thinking?" Throughout our relationship, I had worked in a traditional middle school, taught graduate-level courses, trained middle and high school teachers for NYCTF, and researched charter schools extensively. Spending days interviewing and researching innovative models such as The MET School, MATCH, and KIPP, I felt that I had a solid idea of cutting-edge high school models.

Interviews for leadership programs ensued. In the middle of my interviewing process, I became incredibly ill. I knew the leadership program was right for me, so I convinced the doctor to turn off the IV and take off the hospital bracelet for one day—just long enough for me to drive into New York City, interview, and make it back to the hospital for treatment. I still don't know how I made it through that interview.

Less than three weeks later, I received the much-awaited acceptance letter. We had two months to move back to New York City. My husband would leave his stable career and search for another industry job, simply to help me actualize my dream.

During the program, we learned about then-chancellor Joel Klein's initiative to create new small schools throughout New York City. My team and I were asked to write a proposal, and were offered the opportunity to submit it to the Department of Education. We were asked by the College Board to partner in developing a school for international affairs.

After months of preparation, we had one shot to get the school approved. A panel of ten interviewers questioned our ideas and implementation plans for thirty minutes. I had never been more nervous in my life. Yet I knew I was where I needed to be—going big or going home.

Two days after Christmas, I received a call telling me that our Queens Collegiate's proposal had been accepted and that we would be given space in a landmarked school, on the top of a hill, in the heart of the most diverse New York borough: Queens.

As a child in Pennsylvania, I dreamt of a secondary school where students learned world languages and cultural traditions, and communicated on a global scale. As the principal of Queens Collegiate, I strive daily for global collaboration, rigorous academic programs, and a community that embraces all members and their unique traits. It did not come without intensive work, dedication, and a dream. The constant belief to "go big or go home" kept me going. Really, who sets out to design and lead a school at age thirty-two? Yet I do not see any other way.

Task 4: Fill the Box of Beauty Ointment (Learn to Say No)

For the fourth and final task, Aphrodite orders Psyche to undertake a hazardous journey through what is described in mythology as the underworld (I'd probably refer to it as the vale of tears) and fill a box with beauty ointment. This task is more than the traditional hero's test, for Psyche is told she will encounter people on her way who will importune her and to whom she must say no in order to fulfill her mission.

Let me illustrate.

Whenever I attend Parent-Teacher Organization (PTO) meetings I seem to volunteer for something, a big something. One year I volunteered to chair the Cultural Enrichment Committee, the next year to be the Hospitality Chair. Here's how things unfold.

The PTO president asks for volunteers. Amidst the ensuing uncomfortable silence, my brain starts to run the script: good mothers volunteer at their children's school. Over the years, I have volunteered far less than most because of my work schedule. I want to be a good mother and I want others to think I'm a good mother. Impulsively, compulsively even, I volunteer. Five minutes later, I regret it.

Have you ever said yes when you really wanted to say no? Learning to say no, and thus exercise choice, is Psyche's fourth and final task.

Setting a goal and pursuing it in the face of requests for help from others is especially difficult for women whose lives are focused on caregiving. And yet, as we say no, we learn to set boundaries, to exercise choice, and, paradoxically, to more capably say yes to relatedness and nurturing.

In his book *The Power of a Positive No*, William Ury writes:

I learned [the importance of saying no] early on in my career from the...extraordinarily successful investor Warren Buffett. Over breakfast one day, he confided in me that the secret to creating his fortune was his ability to say No. "I sit there and look at investment proposals all day. I say No, No, No, No, No, No—until I see one that is exactly what I am looking for. And then I say Yes. All I have to do is say Yes a few times in my life and I've made my fortune. Every important Yes requires a thousand Nos."

For women, these thousand nos are particularly nettlesome because they require us to move from the mindset of either/or to both/and to do what Ury describes as "marrying the two most fundamental words in the language: Yes and No. Yes is the key word of connection. No is the key word of protection. Psyche embarks on a hero's journey by saying yes to Eros. Psyche says no to others to say yes to herself and to her loved ones. As Ury states, the "secret to standing up for yourself and what you need without destroying precious relationships is to marry the two." I love these words attributed to Oprah Winfrey: "We can't ever REALLY say yes, until we learn to say no."

As Psyche completes these four tasks, she learns to sort through and prioritize her possibilities, to learn when and how to obtain power without selling her soul, to achieve goals and delegate, and to say no. Yet, despite all she achieves, her basic feminine nature remains unchanged. For she never would have undertaken this journey, risking everything, had it not been for someone she loves. When she completes these tasks, she has truly grown up.

In 2008, I went to my first Boston Celtics basketball game. Although I was a spectator, I didn't feel like one. My friend Kim had purchased four tickets, and she subsequently invited me, along with two other up-and-coming professional women to the game. We watched the game (the Celtics won), but in between the winning shots we got to know one another. We shared our dreams and the "doing" of them. We may not have been dribbling the ball down the court, but we were playing our own game of ball and cheering one another on. In all the important ways, we were players in the game—our game. I am still very much a cheerleader and I love that aspect of myself. However, dreaming has taught me how and when to throw down my pom-poms and get in the game.

TRULY GROWING UP...

Throw down your pom-poms and get in the game.

- How does putting yourself at the center of your life help you to dream?
- The next time you tell someone about something you've accomplished or vice versa, is it possible that you're actually asking for something, such as recognition or help? Keeping in mind Dr. Fels's work, perhaps you can help someone else. Ask what you can do to help.
- After you've thrown down your pom-poms for a time, have you noticed that when you pick them back up, you are ready to cheer others on all the more heartily?
- How can understanding the Psyche myth help us understand that dreaming is essential?
- When we dream, set goals, and achieve them despite distractions, are we not temporarily saying no to our loved ones so that we can say yes in a more profound and emphatic way?

4

TO SHOW CHILDREN
HOW TO DREAM

More than once when I've wanted a girlfriend to go somewhere with me or do something, I've cavalierly said, "Just get a babysitter." Or, "Why can't your husband watch them for a few hours?"

When my friends didn't give in to my pleading, I just couldn't understand why. It seemed so simple, so straightforward, especially since we could all rattle on about the importance of "taking time for ourselves." Yet with ample opportunity to get away for a few hours, these women declined to do so.

Then one day, while serving as the director of public relations for my church in Greater Boston, I received a call from the Washington bureau of the British Broadcasting Company (BBC). When reporters wanted to meet with members of my church, it was my job to make that happen. The BBC called on Monday and wanted interviews on Wednesday. Ordinarily that wouldn't have been a problem, but I was on my way out of town. I needed to delegate the task, but to my surprise I found it extremely difficult to do. I felt guilty for imposing on another committee member. After all, she was busy too. But I also felt fear—fear that if I didn't do "my job," my identity would disappear.

Each of us has an identity, probably several. These identities are ways of defining who we are—daughter, sister, mother, wife, doctor, investment professional, etc. Although we are each many people, so to speak, we typically have a primary identity that's related to whatever we spend most of our time doing. Because most of my past two decades have been career-focused, my identity is centered on myself as a worker. When I get stuff done in the community or workplace, I shore up my identity. In turn, when I delegate or give away those tasks, I feel as if I'm weakening that identity.

The paradox is that unless I'm willing to let go of some of my can-do identity, there isn't room for me to develop other pieces of myself—like the mothering piece of me I wanted to develop. (This piece was, by the way, part of the reason I took a leave from my Wall Street career.) As H.G. Wells said, "You have learned something. That always feels at first as if you had lost something."

I believe each of us confronts this paradox at one time or another. In order to find another piece of who we are, we may need to discard a little bit of who we are right now. In confronting this conundrum, I have found this metaphor from Alyson Jenkins, a stay-at-home mother living in Japan, quite powerful.

Alyson Jenkins: *Be Your Own Batman*

One of my dad's friends always said, "What's better than one Meidell?" My sister and I would grin, shouting in unison, "Two Meidells!" In our small California town, I was Brooke's little sister, one of Pat's daughters, and Mr. Meidell's youngest girl (although people often thought my dad was my grandpa).

I knew where I belonged, but my life felt solely defined by my relationships—by being someone else's something.

Moving to a new town as a teenager and later going to college in a different state was an opportunity to develop my own identity, but when I married and eventually had children, I felt my identity again slipping. I'm no longer Brooke's little sister, but I'm Mackay or Grant's mom or David's wife. Even before I married, because I have a master's in clinical social work, my life was focused on helping others, pushing for social change. While I love and cherish all of these roles, they've made it difficult to develop an independent identity—to be *my* something.

Thanks to Whitney's inspiration, thinking about being the hero of my own journey has really changed my life. As a woman and social worker I am, by nature and by training, a helper, like Batman's Robin. It's been easy to be someone else's something. But realizing I can also be Batman—*my* something— has been life-altering.

I've never felt like a hero. No single-bound leaping here. However, when I look back on my past through this new lens, I see small acts of heroism. My first Batman experiences were leaving the city of my birth, going to college, obtaining degrees, and getting married, to name a few events.

Before all this hero talk, I would have said it ended there. Now I think that was just the beginning. Learning to be my own Batman began in earnest after having my first baby. Being a stay-at-home mom to a newborn was frustrating and, truth be told, a little tedious at times.

I looked to the women around me to learn something new. Judy taught me to knit. Ann taught me to sew. Stacey showed me the art of bookbinding. Heidi passed on her knowledge of jewelry making, and I did end up selling my jewelry to boutiques. I taught myself to cook. I researched recipes and tried out new foods. And with some inspiration from my brother, I ran my first marathon. This was all just in the first year. When I look closely enough, I see in my actions small, Batman-like heroism, acts that helped me find space in my life for me.

As women we often identify heroics with the rescue missions we orchestrate. Who else but us can fly in and whip up a healthy meal from the paltry ingredients left in the fridge, complete with hors d'oeuvres and dessert for the friends who drop in? Who else can negotiate with insurgents to rescue an ill-fated art project from the grips of devious younger siblings? We can encounter and restore order to a flooded laundry room and fix an unintentionally broken lamp. In my Robin "helper" world, this is a typical Monday night, but it's my Batman moments that provide the fuel.

I love being Robin, riding along in my husband and children's sidecars, championing all their efforts to move forward, but when I also see myself as Batman, with my husband and children riding along in my sidecar, I'm happier, so much happier and, not coincidentally, a much better Robin.

As Alyson teaches, when we learn to become both Robin and Batman, we open the door to our dreams, and not coincidentally, we open the door to our children's dreams as well. We need to recognize that, in addition to the fear of assuming new identities, we must also consider the guilt, guilt that we are somehow being bad when we do something for ourselves. Elizabeth Keeler's dreams have taken unexpected turns, from piano performance major, to a Master's degree in English, to her current pursuit of an MBA. She shares her mixed feelings of guilt and exhilaration as she has moved from one dream to the next, sailing uncharted waters.

Elizabeth Keeler: *Confessions of a Cliff-Jumper*

I don't like extreme sports and I secretly despise people who fling themselves off cliffs in the name of leisure. I take paranoid care of my body. But, sometimes, when I ponder my life, I think I might be living my own version of insanity—call it "vocational cliff-jumping." My secret resume includes things as disparate as "pianist," "lab chemist," "dancer," and "businesswoman." I am constantly jumping headlong into the deep end of some new professional endeavor. Let me further damage my credibility: I have moved twenty times to thirteen cities in four countries in three continents attending six universities in ten years. Peripatetic, you might say. "Geographic fix-it-itis" my friend's mom diagnosed. "You think moving from one thing to another will fix everything." I imagine the people speaking at my funeral saying things like: "She was confused." Or, "A nice girl, but her internal compass was way off."

I often question myself as I embark on yet another life change. What is wrong with me? Why can't I stay put? Confusion and self-doubt have been a part of every transition. Last year, as I was contemplating forging ahead with my MBA, the questions started again: When and where will I find my bliss? This time I got an answer, and it shocked me. You are living it, the voice came from deep, deep inside me. Pause. Light bulb. With sudden clarity I knew I was living my dream in total perfection: I am a self-decreed explorer. I envisioned myself wearing a captain's hat as I steered my lone ship across the tumultuous waters of the Atlantic.

While I admit there is fear associated with doing something outrageously new, fear is not my greatest deterrent to risk taking. My past life as a musician was like a lifetime vaccination against fear. I have yet to do anything as terrifying as play a Bach fugue for Professor Engle, who was known, on occasion, to mime cutting off my head. I may experience terror frequently, but it's more like an old, pesky friend. No, my greatest deterrent, by far, is guilt. Guilt has accompanied every life change I've made. It's as if there are voices telling me that changing makes me fickle, weak, or abnormal. Perhaps it's the age-old view that incontinence and irrationality are bound up in my femininity. Changing my mind is weak, a modern-day instance of fainting in my corset. The proper thing to do is to be still, stable, responsible. Don't change, don't move, be dependable, be who you've always been, be found in the same space as before. Sometimes guilt is justified, but I have searched my soul about the wrongs of cliff-jumping, and I believe the guilt is ill-founded. If I had acted in perfect accordance with my inherited social conscience, I would be living in rural Canada celebrating my twelve-year wedding anniversary with my husband, cows, dogs, and kids. That may be right for some, but it would have been wrong for me, a sure recipe for socially-guilt-free misery. So what's the deal with my guilt? Perhaps there are evolutionary reasons for the guilt of adventure, but one thing is for sure: the flip side of the guilt-coin is stagnation. To me, that's the real danger. I asked Google and it confirmed my suspicions: "The person who risks nothing, does nothing, has nothing, is nothing, and becomes nothing. [She] may avoid suffering and sorrow, but [she] simply cannot learn and feel and change and grow and love and live." (Leo Buscaglia)

So, while I am perplexed by the guilt, ever-present as it is, the Captain in me insists I sail in spite of it. This week's expedition was to enroll in the advanced private equity class offered next term. As a classmate graciously pointed out, it's laughable how little business I have being there. However, what I know from being an experienced jumper is that after terror comes exhilaration, and if I'm lucky, ecstasy—the ultimate reward. To be clear, I am not promoting that people change jobs every year for the rest of their lives (heaven forbid). I am merely shamelessly advocating headlong, plummeting, frontier-busting, head-shaking, free-falling adventure, however that looks, because it's worth it. I don't know about you, but I intend to keep up my dirty little habit of cliff-jumping for a very long time, even at the risk of a confusing epitaph on my tombstone.

Women often think of themselves as a safe harbor, especially within the context of family life. But it's just as important to be a ship, especially one that can navigate new territory. When we leave the dock and seek our dreams, we can better teach our children, our friends, our colleagues how to navigate the world.

AVOIDING AN UNLIVED LIFE

In the film adaptation of Susan Minot's novel *Evening*, the main character, Ann Grant, is on her deathbed. A flashback shows her in her early twenties, during a time she believed she could achieve all of her dreams, which included having a happy marriage and a successful singing career. As the flashbacks progress, we learn that Ann's life, in the words of famed psychiatrist Carl Jung, was "unlived." She married badly two times, and her singing career never materialized.

Ann's daughter Constance tries to live her mother's unfulfilled dream of having a happy marriage; ostensibly she has, although her demeanor suggests otherwise, and she completely neglects following her bliss. Meanwhile, another daughter, Nina, fails in four careers (including a stint as a go-go dancer), and both happiness and meaningful relationships remain elusive.

When Ann left her life unlived, her daughters unwittingly tried to live it for her. Ann's daughters became the keeper of her dreams rather than of their own. Carl Jung wrote, "Nothing has a stronger influence psychologically on...children than the unlived life of the parent." It doesn't have to be that way.

When Ann is asked to single out a moment of true happiness, she vividly recalls a rehearsal for a singing gig three decades earlier. As Ann sang, five-year-old Constance sat with her mom's accompanist. In that moment Ann was attending to both of her dreams—her relationships and her singing. She was happy.

Attending to multiple dreams at the same time is certainly harder than attending to one or the other. But if by multitasking our dreams we can enable our children to keep theirs, isn't it worth doing?

MULTITASKING OUR DREAMS

We can see positive effects of multitasking dreams, of alternating between being the ship and safe harbor in the life of Nan Hunter, and the founder of a joyous, child-centered private school that began with staging a play in her backyard in 1968.

Nan Hunter: *The Dreams That Didn't Wait*

In 1962, my husband urged me to come up with an "after the children (grew to be eight children in thirteen years) leave home and you don't have anything to do" life plan. I promptly began to think, and in about two days I had a dream. I would start a children's theater where children learned how to act and had the joy and pleasure of giving the gift of performance to their friends and neighbors.

It's 1967. We're in San Jose, California, with three little children. We live in a little yellow house on Whitemarsh Court in a neighborhood full of young families. Somewhere in the gene pool of life I received the energy gene for about ten people. Today's noted child-watchers describe this as hyperactive.

However, this energy gave me the drive to turn an idea into a dream and a dream into a do it. Summer was quiet, very quiet. Why wait until my children were grown to begin my drama school? So I wrote a simple play, made up some songs to familiar tunes, and in our backyard in 1968 I held my first drama workshop with twenty neighborhood children.

That fall our first child entered kindergarten and I began the journey of looking through the wise eyes of a mother at what happened in those big places called schools. To my dismay, schools didn't focus on children. They looked at programs, measured progress by testing, and taught a limited curriculum consisting of math, reading, and social studies. They had gifted programs for the gifted, measured by their abilities in math and reading and thinking skills. Rather than picket, storm the fort, or burn down the building, I thought, "Someday I'm going to start a school." For thirteen years I shared this dream with friends, teachers, and family. Many laughed, smiled their upside-down smiles, and tried to discourage me.

"You'll never do that, Nan, you've got too many children."

"Don't you think you should just stay home and take care of what you've already got to do?"

"Where will you ever find a place to do it?"

In the eyes of the public I looked pretty disorganized and more than a little fractured. Their doubts doubled my determination to do it and in my heart I KNEW MY DREAM WOULD COME TRUE.

It's 1981. Our last child enters kindergarten. In December, the San Jose Unified School District announces that they will close nine of their campuses at the end of the school year, one of which was Henderson, five minutes from my house, a peaceful little neighborhood, a perfect location.

It was time.

In February of 1982 I sent a press release to the *San Jose Mercury News* announcing that a busy mother of eight children was opening a school that fall. One hundred hopeful people called. I had perma-grin all day.

There were no buildings, no books, no teachers, and no uniforms. But over the next six months families poured into our bare living room and sat on folding chairs as I painted the picture of a school where there would be "Gifted education for every child, because every child is gifted." This dream school included drama, art, science, and foreign language beginning in kindergarten.

I interviewed teachers, and promised them jobs. I picked out a curriculum and ordered books that I didn't have to pay for until school started. Two weeks before the promised opening of the school I signed a lease for what would become Almaden Country School. Parents paid full tuition in advance, so we had the money to lease furniture and pay for the books.

Opening day in September of 1982 is still bright in my memory. One hundred ninety little boys and girls from kindergarten to sixth grade marched onto our shiny campus dressed in gingham jumpers or navy shorts and light blue shirts. Our teachers all wore gingham aprons and there was a bright red apple on every desk.

For twenty-eight years now, we have produced about twelve plays a year at Almaden Country School. I have directed or produced "A Christmas Carol" at least twenty-five times in our little auditorium. I also hold Grandma's Camp Summer Theater with my thirty-five grandchildren.

My next dream is to have a theater for the neighborhood on our farm—which I am in the process of building. You'll find me there at Christmas with snow and sleigh bells, surrounded by urchins, ghosts, and the spirit of Christmas Present, and dreaming with my grandchildren.

In pursuing her dreams, Nan Hunter has not only modeled for her eight children how to achieve their dreams, she has created an environment in which thousands of children are learning to dream.

ATTENDING TO RELATIONSHIPS AND OURSELVES SIMULTANEOUSLY

As I read Nan's story, I thought of one of my favorite children's books, *The Country Bunny and the Little Gold Shoes,* a book not coincidentally introduced to me by Nan's daughter Kathleen. Written by DuBose Heyward and illustrated by Marjorie Flack in 1939, the book begins with the sentence: "We hear of the Easter Bunny who comes each Easter Day before sunrise to bring eggs for boys and girls, so we think there is only one."

Following are a few lines from the story that illustrate why we need to dream for ourselves, why we need to dream for our children, and how we can attend to our dreams while also attending to our relationships and ourselves.

1. *Some day I shall grow up to be an Easter Bunny—you wait and see!*

   Nearly all little girls have a strong sense of what they want to do, and their "Who I am." This little girl bunny was determined to become the Easter Bunny.

2. *By and by she had a husband and then one day ... there were twenty-one Cottontail babies to take care of.*

As we grow up, we sift through seeds of possibilities in the face of conflicting feelings and competing loyalties. Although the little bunny dreamed of becoming the Easter Bunny, she also dreamed of marrying and having twenty-one Cottontail babies. She made a choice, and as you read on you learn she honored her choice.

3. *One day, when her children stopped being babies and were little girl and boy bunnies, she called them to her and said, "Now we are going to have some fun."*

As the bunny's children grow, she helps them achieve the confidence and capacity to dream their own dreams by involving them and delegating to them. Her offspring are competent, capable bunnies.

4. *You have proved yourself to be not only wise and kind, and swift, but also very clever. Come to the Palace tomorrow afternoon, and you shall be my fifth Easter Bunny.*

As a character, the Country Bunny illustrates that life can be a both/and proposition—she can attend to those whom she loves and to herself. She is wise and kind, and deeply connected to those she loves. She is also swift, clever, courageous, and open to possibilities. By seeking out possibilities, the bunny teaches her children to do the same. By delegating, she gives her children the skills to open doors to their own possibilities.

We dream because dreaming is who we are. In dreaming, we teach our children how to dream.

LETTING OUR CHILDREN DREAM

As parents, we sometimes struggle to remember that our children are creatures independent of ourselves and that their dreams are not always the dreams we might have for them. Kristine Haglund, who holds a bachelor's and master's degree in German literature, experienced this process of acceptance with her first son, Peter, whose dreams are very different from her own.

Kristine Haglund: *Through the Mist of Expectations*

I remember watching my firstborn son sleep. Despite the haze of exhaustion that blanketed my fragile consciousness, I didn't want to miss a single one of those newborn sleep-smiles. I remember feeling pangs of—what?—jealousy? betrayal? when his eyes flitted back and forth under the blue-veined lids. He was dreaming, his infant neurons visiting worlds I could not see. I intuited, though I could not have given words to the feeling, that he was leaving me, continuing the long farewell that began the moment his tiny, slick body escaped mine.

My own grief at that first agonized separation was the part of motherhood that most surprised me, that surprises me even now when my delight in the unfolding of my children's personalities is shadowed by the sometimes desperate wish for them to stop, to please, please wait for me, to keep holding my hand, to let me come with them. And the sweet longing to enter their dreams with them has, I fear, an uglier shadow side—I want them to stay with me in *my* dreams.

As a child, I had vivid and specific dreams about the family I would have when I grew up. I was a musician and would-be conductor, so I planned to have ten children: a string quartet, then a pianist, then a wind quintet. All their names would end in "yn"—Megyn, Justyn, Robyn, Eryn...(what can I say? It was the 70s!). I filled an old lesson planner from my mother's days as a schoolteacher with elaborate practice schedules—I drew up plans for a dream house with shared bedrooms for the children, a big reading room with no furniture but bookshelves and giant pillows on the floor, and three practice rooms at the far corners of the house so that all of this practicing could happen simultaneously. I read up on Crock-Pot cooking because I knew that after-school time would be very, very busy (all of the children would play at least one sport and be heavily involved in church and community service, too, of course). I wish I were exaggerating!

I was slightly more sane by the time I actually became pregnant, and first trimester nausea made me think that, really, the Brahms horn trios are very nice, very nice indeed...But it still remained the task of my first baby to help me let go.

Even before he was born, he had his own agenda. I had to be induced twice, because he *would* come in his own sweet time. We had planned to name him Benjamin, but his father and I both knew the instant we saw him that his name was Peter, a name which was on neither of our short lists, and which we discovered only later was the name of my great-great-great-great grandfather. He was teaching me the lesson I needed most of all—that every child is a miraculous being, who comes (in the gorgeous words of Stephen Spender) "from corridors of light where the hours are suns/Endless and singing." They are no more my creatures than the flowers or mountains or oceans are mine. As I fell in love with him, he taught me how to love, how to make safe space for his dreams and share mine as gifts rather than wielding them as weapons.

As it turned out, he has an autism spectrum disorder, and my calendar was filled with doctor and therapist appointments instead of music lessons. His dreams are of tools and gears and gadgets and impossibly complicated machines (once I found him curled up in bed with a pair of bolt-cutters!), and he hates to talk about them almost as much as I love, love, love to talk, talk, talk about mine in florid detail. The bridge between my dream world and his is tenuous and rickety—the winds blow hard between us, and we both stumble a lot. But sometimes, on clear days when love burns off the mist of my expectations, I catch glimpses of his horizons, more beautiful than I could have dreamed.

Kristine expresses so beautifully that when our love for a child overrides our expectations, we can bridge the divide between our hopes and dreams and our child's. I also firmly believe that when we get on with our own lives, leaving no part of our lives unlived, we are better able to allow our children to live theirs. I've experienced this in my own life. Here's a story from my parenting annals, written when my son was ten:

"Mom, why are you discouraging me?" asked my ten year-old with frustration. Within a day of auditioning for a local play, and not yet knowing if any of us would be cast, I found myself saying, "You know, David, there aren't very many parts for boys your age, so don't be disappointed if you aren't picked."

The words had just tumbled out, and rather than my son finding what I said comforting, he asked why I was being so unsupportive. After all, one of our family rules is "Johnsons support each other."

"But, but, but..." I began to defend my words to myself, I'm just trying to protect him. I don't want him to be disappointed. Really? Protect him or protect me?

"Mom, why are you discouraging me?"

Here I am, day after day, continually encouraging everyone I come in contact with, especially women, to "dare to dream."

But to my child I say, "Don't be disappointed if you aren't picked."

If I'm saying things like that to my children but not to my friends and colleagues, the problem must be at least partly about me. To paraphrase Tolstoy: When it comes to family, we sometimes don't know where we end and others begin.

That makes me wonder: Did my mother say such discouraging things to me? (And her mother to her, and so on down through the generations?) When we heard our parents utter some variation on the theme of "don't be disappointed," did any of us hear "I love you"? Or did we instead hear, "I don't believe in you. I don't really think you can do this"?

Fortunately, I had the opportunity for a do-over just a few months later when David wanted to go to a casting call for the PBS show *Fetch! with Ruff Ruffman,* an *Apprentice*-style program featuring ten- to fourteen-year-olds. I knew the odds of his being chosen were small. Not only were about 350 kids auditioning, David had just turned ten. If I were the casting director, I would want the cast to skew older, not younger.

But because I'm learning, I didn't say a word. It was *so* hard. I had to gate the words that wanted to tumble out, begging to sally forth, as if they were caged dogs eager for a run. But I said nothing, and I went one better. Instead of saying, "You might be disappointed," I said, "David, I'm happy you're figuring out what kinds of things you like, and that you took the initiative to go after what you wanted."

We might not have heard words of encouragement from our parents, but we can do things differently; the children in our lives can hear these words from us. And, oh, will they ever hear them, because mum's the word.

Abigail Adams wrote, "O Blindness to the future kindly given that each may fill the circle marked by Heaven." When we dream our own dreams, rather than sending messages to our children about ourselves, and quite possibly our unfulfilled dreams, we can patiently be blind. In allowing them to focus on their own lives, we are trusting that our children will "fill their circle marked by Heaven." Rather than living through our children, we can become witnesses to the lives they choose to live.

DREAMING BY EXAMPLE...

You have learned something. That always feels at first as if you had lost something.

> —H.G. Wells, nineteenth-century English science fiction writer

- Is there something you've wanted to do recently, if only for a few hours, that you just wouldn't let yourself do?
- If you find yourself repeatedly wanting to do this thing, will you promise yourself to do it next time, knowing full well that you'll be just a little bit uncomfortable? (After a few days, do you still feel uncomfortable, or just a little bit happier?)
- How can learning to be Batman help us be a better Robin?
- If you were to write a letter to your children, could you identify two or three things you *do now* to help restore your sense of self? If you can, what are they? If you can't, what would those things be?
- What does it look like to say no to your loved ones in the near-term so you can say yes to them long-term?

What the mother sings to the cradle goes all the way down to the coffin.

> —Henry Ward Beecher, nineteenth-century
> clergyman and abolitionist

- What are we saying to our children that is not about them, but about us? What are we saying to our children that *is* about them? What are they hearing?
- How can taking on our own challenges and seeing our own possibilities help our children take on and see their own?
- As mothers, we are our daughters' examples of how to dream. If we don't dream, how will they?

PART TWO

Dream

Boldly Finding Your Dreams

Within your heart, keep one still, secret
spot where dreams may go.

—*Louise Driscoll, twentieth-century American poet*

We've asked and answered the question, why dream? And perhaps you've always been willing to dare, but you've never been able to precisely put your finger on what your dream is. Or you've achieved some dreams and are wondering, what's next? Maybe you are finding that several of your dearest dreams are colliding. In this section, we'll go through the process around deciphering your current dream, sharing examples of other women who are figuring this out for themselves. You will practice casting yourself as the leading character in your life, and we'll discuss clearing a space for your dream. We will then begin to mine for your possibilities among your innate talents, competencies, background, and beliefs. You'll likely discover that your next dream isn't somewhere over the rainbow, but rather right under your feet. To conclude this section, we'll discuss sorting through and prioritizing competing desires. This may mean you need to realign your dreams to fit your current circumstances, or you may find that your aspirations aren't yet in step with your genius.

5

BE THE HERO OF YOUR STORY

Having established that it is essential to dream, you may be thinking, "I'm ready to dream. But I have no idea what my dream is!" Some of us know exactly what we want; some of us don't. More of us have a nascent sense, but the dream remains vague or amorphous and will require concerted effort on our part to give it definition. In asking ourselves the following questions, we can help our dreams take shape:

- What did you like to do as a child?
- What makes you happy?
- What are some of your most difficult life experiences?
- How do your core beliefs help or hinder your dreams?
- Might your dream need some resizing—down or up?

As we answer these questions, the contours of our dream will emerge. We can then begin to explore our possibilities and try out different dreams.

PREPARING TO DREAM

Before we dive deep into questions about the details of our dreams, which we'll do in this section, it is important to do a little prep work, a pregame warm-up, as it were, of figuratively throwing down our pom-poms, so we can get our head and heart in the game. When we have become accustomed to sidelining ourselves, getting in the game and casting ourselves as a key player in our story will not be easy.

So let's start by talking about reality TV. I'll admit here, without embarrassment, that I'm a fan. It began with *American Idol*, and more recently I've become hooked on *So You Think You Can Dance*, *Project Runway*, and *The Next Food Network Star*. The mythologist Joseph Campbell, while not writing about reality TV directly, provides an explanation for this genre's success when he says: "A hero ventures forth from the world of common day into a region of supernatural wonder: fabulous forces are there encountered and a decisive victory is won: the hero comes back from this mysterious adventure with the power to bestow boons on his fellow man."

Isn't this what happens on reality TV? Right before our eyes we see people who are hoping to be called to adventure, to be chosen for a hero's journey, and to obtain the boon. As we watch and vote for our favorites, we find pieces of ourselves mirrored in the contestants, feeling as if we, too, are on the hero's journey.

While it's true that all of the finalists can sing or dance, sew or cook, the contestants often move us simply because they don't seem to know how talented they are. As we watch contestants with self-doubt and raw talent acknowledged by the judges and the voters, we muse to ourselves, "Maybe I don't know how magnificent I am, either." If that contestant has been discovered—or chosen—perhaps we can be, too. Even though, in the end, there is only one winner, we are inspired by seeing so many heroes move to the center of their lives, conquering fear and insecurity.

CASTING OURSELVES AS THE HERO

As we begin to claim a central place in our lives, we can begin to discover our dreams. If we tend to move ourselves to the sidelines and live through the dreams of others, dreaming our own dreams will require a paradigm shift. We can trigger this shift, preparing for our possibilities, by telling stories about ourselves, stories in which we are the central character. We can also immerse ourselves in stories about women, real or fictional, who dare to follow their dreams.

One of the places I practice telling stories in which I'm at the center is on my blog. I started *Dare to Dream* because I believed I had something to say, but also because I wanted to find my voice. In finding myself and becoming the hero of my story, I hope to encourage other women to do the same.

Being the hero will look very different for you than it does for me. Although each of our journeys will have the same central elements, the details will differ. As we begin to tell stories in which we see ourselves as the hero, we begin to believe that what we do matters. Take the story of Athelia "CK" LeSueur, the cofounder of Shabby Apple (shabbyapple.com). Upon graduation from college, she had intended to work in international development. Athelia's opportunity to move to the center of her life ironically came when significant health problems curtailed her plan to work abroad and she had to move home for a time.

Athelia LeSueur: *Fortunate Frustrations*

Splat. I looked up at a laughing audience and a stunned dance partner. Falling in the middle of a performance? I could get over it. But dancing through my senior project with a hurt leg? How?

"Work with what you have; utilize your limitations," Professor Moses told me. Yeech! Trite advice. But, now that I couldn't jump, I decided to do the entire piece with a part of my body connected to the wall. The dance remains my favorite.

In high school, I put in writing that I wanted to be a fashion designer; unfortunately, I couldn't sew. I tried. Once. I designed and sewed costumes for my high school dance concert. To the chagrin of one dancer...and the delight of the boys in the audience...her costume fell apart mid-performance! That, I thought, ended my fashion career.

Work with what you have: three years ago, I had finished graduate school, but health problems forced me to move home to live with my parents. I had studied women's rights and international development, but I couldn't find a relevant project in Utah...Frustration. Nor could I work for long hours at a time. This limitation forced me to focus and work efficiently.

My co-founder Emily McCormick had her own set of frustrations. With a new baby, she no longer wanted to pursue a full-time career in marketing, but still wanted to keep a hand in marketing. As we brainstormed possibilities, reminiscing about how we enjoyed dressing our high school friends in cute clothes, we decided to start a line of clothing, focusing on dresses.

Utilize your limitations: because we had limited experience, we did research, and lots of it (our two favorite books were *The McGraw-Hill Guide to Starting Your Own Business* by Stephen Harper and *The Fashion Designer Survival Guide* by

Mary Gehlhar), but there was still so much we didn't know, industry jargon, for instance. I remember listening carefully to what store owners said at retail shows, but one factory owner later asked me where I had received my training because my "phrasing was so unique!"

Our limited experience also meant we didn't understand all of the fashion business protocol; this actually worked to our advantage. For example, we didn't know we were supposed to hire an expensive wholesaler to represent us to buyers, a task that most wholesalers do not do well, causing many companies to fail. And because we knew we bought our own clothes online, we simply bypassed the wholesalers and opened a dot-com store.

Another limitation that accrued to our benefit was lack of funds. As a small, undercapitalized start-up, the one manufacturer who would help us gave us only two fabric choices: cotton poplin and poly/spandex jersey. Because each seam, pleat, button, or pin tuck in a dress cost extra money to produce, and we didn't have money, out of necessity, we kept our designs simple, making the design process easier, faster, and better.

We experienced many "blips" in manufacturing before we perfected our process. One such blip involved Emily and me personally ripping the buttons off five hundred incorrectly sewn dresses. Another involved a manufacturer who "changed its mind" about producing dresses two days before it was supposed to ship hundreds of dresses we'd presold. Not all frustrations are fortunate.

As for limitations around design, Emily and I agreed easily, but convincing the manufacturers we really did want our dresses to have sleeves, higher necklines, and hemlines at least to the knee was not easy. As frustrating as this was, it helped us define our brand and eventually get more publicity for Shabby Apple.

Everyone has frustrations in life. Some frustrations and limitations can't be overcome. But even with these constraints, and quite possibly because of them, I have been fortunate to do something that I love.

When Athelia couldn't pursue her original dream of working in international development, she discovered a new dream, a new adventure, and though the road she and her partner traveled in creating their business was often bumpy, she has certainly achieved the hero's boon—Athelia's passion for simple, beautiful clothes has been rewarded in the tremendous success of Shabby Apple. The opportunity for Madeleine Walburger, a mother of four and a health care consultant to the pharmaceutical industry, to move to the center of her story came as a college freshman. Her goal: to beat Stanford's triple-jump record.

Madeleine Walburger: *Perchance to Dream*

Hop-skip-and-a-jump. For more than half of my undergraduate experience, I spent countless hours developing my abilities as a triple-jumper on the Stanford University track and field team. As an incoming freshman, school was my top priority, but I was also eager to see what I could achieve with collegiate coaching and year-round training. In high school I had a fantastic coach, but I could only devote about three months a year to the sport. I leapt at the chance to accelerate both my intellectual and athletic abilities.

I started practice a week after school began and soon learned of a long-standing Stanford record for a freshman triple jump: 39' 1". The mark was further than I had ever jumped, but I considered it within the realm of possibility. I remember peddling home from practice that day, ice bags wrapped around my shins. I ran up the two flights of concrete stairs to my dorm room, where I emblazoned the distance in pen and highlighter on an index card. I posted the card facing my desk and my bed. Here was a soaring dream to spur on my hours of running, jumping, lifting, and competing.

I enjoyed the training, the competing, and the camaraderie, but with few personal successes among us, it was a long eight months for me and for my jumper teammates. More than once I was tempted to pull down my index card before the season was over, but I never did.

I'm not a natural dreamer and with this realization, a question formed: "Why? Why is it hard for me to dream?" I believe I found an answer, or rather two answers.

I'm an analytical decision maker. I aim high and think big with one foot firmly grounded in faith and the other in reality. I consider the variables involved in my decision, seek providential guidance, and then I try and make the best choice, assume the best attitude, and/or map out the best course of action for myself and my family. I seldom weigh personal likes or interests as variables. My approach is not perfect, but it has produced many strong and happy results.

I don't like to fail. When I identify a dream, there is a possibility I may not accomplish it. So I sometimes hedge my bets. I stay in my comfort zone by aiming high only in those areas where I know I'm strong or where I have a solid infrastructure of support. Otherwise, I don't even make an attempt.

I want to learn how to dream. I want to listen to my instincts and learn to consider what I love doing regardless of its practicality. I want to learn to value the process and not simply the end. This may not be the season to fully realize many of my aspirations, but I can play with the concept and dream dabble.

Three weeks ago I posted a card on my wall to remind me of my new aspiration. It reads, *"Perchance to Dream—I dare you."*

I put it by my bedroom door, where it fell to the floor twice. I moved it to my bathroom mirror, where it fell onto the counter, behind the toothbrushes.

The metaphor does not escape me. Like gravity's attack on my homemade sign, life's rapid pace, its unexpected diversions, and my insecurities may doggedly attempt to thwart my efforts to see beyond the practical and immediate. Nevertheless, I'm determined to try. I have identified a few personal interests in which I will dabble in the coming year. Here are two.

- Write four unique essays and share them with my "inner circle" of friends. Identify three to five new teaching techniques to develop and apply to my educating responsibilities at my congregation and in my Summer Academy for my children.

My prompt is now duct-taped to the wall.

Back in my college days, after my final meet of the outdoor season, I took down my highlighted triple-jumping goal. I hadn't hit my mark. After devoting so many waking hours to its accomplishment, it stung to not meet such a publicly posted goal. It felt like failure, although in hindsight, I know it wasn't. I had allowed myself to dream.

I still have my 39' 1" index card from my freshman year. It's in a trunk in the garage. I may post it again, next to my new prompt, *"Perchance to Dream—I dare you."*

As Madeleine and Athelia experienced, each of us has the opportunity to become the hero of our story, an opportunity often precipitated by a crisis. We can choose to accept or decline the call. As we embark on our journey we will travel a road fraught with trials, which, if we are to become a hero, we'll struggle through and survive. When we dare to be the hero of our own story, we begin to grow up, to define our dreams, to become more ourselves than ever.

HEARING A WOMAN'S POINT OF VIEW

We can also learn to take the stage by listening to the stories of those who already have. And if you believe, as I do, that women are fundamentally different from men, it's important that we hear women's voices. Unfortunately, so many women, even successful women, refuse to claim a central place in their lives and in their own stories that finding self-assured women within our circle of loved ones can be difficult. It is equally problematic, if not more so, to find strong women's stories within the annals of literature. The Psyche myth and the biblical passages in Proverbs are notable exceptions. Ironically, these stories were written thousands of years ago.

The popular press skews male as well. According to the Annenberg Public Policy Center, only 3 percent of the top positions in mainstream media are held by women. And bylines in the nation's top intellectual and political magazines are heavily male. Meanwhile, according to the *Columbia Journalism Review,* in an analysis of eleven magazines published between October 2003 and May 2005, male-to-female byline ratios ranged from thirteen to one at the *National Review* to seven to one at *Harper's.*

When we become aware of just how many of the media stories we ingest are from a man's point of view, it becomes much easier to understand why we struggle to believe that we as women can dream—and therefore dreaming does require that we dare.

GAINING INSPIRATION FROM
LITERATURE AND FILM

There are some books and films that help me move to the center of my life and, most importantly, inspire me to dream when surrounded by naysayers (including myself). They include:

- *My Grandfather's Blessings* by Rachel Naomi Remen
- *Personal History* by Katharine Graham
- *If You Don't Have Big Breasts, Put Ribbons on Your Pigtails* by Barbara Corcoran
- *The Blue Sweater* by Jacqueline Novogratz
- *Julie and Julia,* a film starring Meryl Streep
- *The Help* by Kathryn Stockett
- *Miss Congeniality II*, a film starring Sandra Bullock

For girls, I'm fond of these titles:

- *The Country Bunny and the Little Gold Shoes* by DuBose Heyward
- *A Wrinkle in Time* by Madeleine L'Engle
- *Matilda* by Roald Dahl
- *A Little Princess* by Frances Hodgson Burnett
- *Secondhand Charm* by Julie Berry
- *Book of a Thousand Days* by Shannon Hale
- *The Sweetness at the Bottom of the Pie* by Alan Bradley

CLAIMING A CENTRAL PLACE IN
STORIES OF BIRTH

One of the best places to mine for stories in which we are central characters is in stories about birth, whether our own or the births of our children. Under what circumstances did we come into the world? What hope was born into the world the day that you and I were born? On the day of our birth, we were the hero. Perhaps that's why birthdays are so important. They remind us that we are heroes of our own stories.

Debra Bingham, DrPH, RN, is a perinatal consultant with more than thirty years of experience. Bingham works with hospital leaders to improve care for mothers and babies and is the president of Lamaze International. Her thoughts on how to improve maternal mortality rates in the United States are quite intriguing, and I believe they have far-reaching implications, which include helping women move to the center of their own stories.

She writes on the *Dare to Dream* blog: "The rates of maternal death and maternal childbirth-related injuries are rising in the United States. In fact, we have not seen maternal mortality rates this high since the early 1970s. In addition, in 2007 the United States was ranked forty-first among developed countries for maternal mortality rates. These negative trends and worsening outcomes do not make sense in a country with so many resources. Why has maternity care become less mother- and newborn-centric, and more hospital-, nurse-, and physician-centric? Why is maternity care costing so much and resulting in such poor outcomes?"

Bingham argues that our beliefs affect behavior: "How women and men discuss the process of pregnancy and birth can have a negative or positive effect on the women that are involved in the discussion. Our words are powerful and either reinforce or undermine the power of women and their bodies."

Bingham suggests we ask ourselves the following questions the next time we talk about childbirth.

- Does your discourse include stories about the power of women?
- Or do the stories shift control away from women and their bodies to other authority figures, such as nurses, physicians, or machines?
- Does your discourse assume that women are physiologically capable of giving birth and nourishing their own children?
- Or does your discourse assume that women's bodies are fundamentally flawed and in need of medical attention and intervention?

Debra Bingham's words are revelatory. As I reflect on her remarks, I see that I shifted much of the locus of control away from me when I had my two children. Her observations are a stark reminder of how deep-seated our inclination is to deflect, to redirect resources away from ourselves. Even when engaged in something that is uniquely a woman's job, we somehow give away our place at the center.

So why not retell the stories of our birth, and of the birth or adoption of our children, in a way that moves us to the center of our story? Why not tell stories in which we claim our power as givers of life, recognizing that our bodies are ingeniously built-to-spec for this precise purpose? Can we, in turn, tell similar stories about giving birth to our dreams? I believe we can. In fact, I know we can. As former British Prime Minister Margaret Thatcher once said, "If you want to get something done, ask a woman."

Discovering and "doing" our dreams requires that we claim a central place in our lives, to accept not only a supporting role but also a leading role. As we practice telling and listening to stories in which we are the lead player or are encouraged to be, we begin to discover who we are and who we want to be. We discover clues to our dreams, and we start to believe that the resources needed to achieve our dreams are ours to have and that, as heroes, they are our birthright.

BECOMING THE MAIN CHARACTER

A hero ventures forth from the world of common day into a region of supernatural wonder: fabulous forces are there encountered and a decisive victory is won: the hero comes back from this mysterious adventure with the power to bestow boons on his fellow man.
   —Joseph Campbell, American folklorist and mythologist

- How does learning to become the hero help you discover your dream?
- Are there elements of the call to adventure, road of trials, and discovery of the boon in your life right now?

You have something that IT has not. This something is your only weapon. But you must find it for yourself.
   —Mrs. Which in *A Wrinkle in Time*, Madeleine L'Engle

- What books and/or films inspire you to dream?
- Do these works help you stick with a dream when you feel discouraged?

All children mythologize their birth. It is a universal trait. You want to know someone? Heart, mind, and soul? Ask him to tell you about when he was born.

—Diane Setterfield, American author

- What is the story of your birth? Are you the youngest? Oldest? Was it a happy time or bittersweet?
- What's the story of the birth or adoption of your children?
- What happens when you claim your rightful place in the bearing of children?
- How can the retelling of your birth stories help give birth to your dreams?

6

MAKE SPACE FOR
YOUR DREAMS

When I left Merrill Lynch to pursue several entrepreneurial ventures (meaning that I, the sole breadwinner, stopped earning money), my family and I downsized from a six-thousand-square-foot home to a townhouse in order to conserve cash. All of our belongings had to fit into a space a quarter of the size we once had. The directive "A place for everything and everything in its place" sounded perfectly doable, but I was overwhelmed. The task felt monolithic. Rather than beginning the work, I ignored it.

A kind friend offered her help. "Let's start by organizing the papers in your upstairs office," she said. "We'll take it one step at a time. We'll do a gross sort first, then a fine sort." With her assistance, I gradually put my papers and files in order.

Big dreams don't intimidate me, but the smallest organizational projects are paralyzing. Perhaps it's the opposite for you. Maybe you instinctively know how and where to store your things, and you do it with style, yet achieving a big dream feels beyond your reach. If so, what I propose is to approach your challenges and dreams one step at a time.

CREATING A PLACE AND A TIME TO DREAM

Step 1. Clear the clutter and create a space where you can dream: this space—or spot or place—can be a desk, an office, your car, or your bed.

Step 2. More importantly, create a space in your day: this space—or time—can be early in the morning, after the kids go to school, while exercising, or late at night. Children make time (or we make them make time) to do homework. We need the same discipline.

In August 2007, I wrote on my blog: "It's been nearly eight months since I started working with Clayton Christensen (a Harvard Business School professor and architect of the framework of disruptive innovation) and his son Matt Christensen on an investment fund, but not until today have I allowed myself to believe it really *will* happen. The feeling came on suddenly, surprisingly. And it wasn't because Clay and I had agreed upon my percentage ownership (we already had) or because an institutional investor expressed interest (which was the case). It was because we'd found office space, and the fund moved from something conceptual, even abstract, to something real. We now had a physical space, a little (very little) corner of the world that had the sole purpose of facilitating the launch of that fund—and one of my dreams. Thinking about that office makes me think about the special places I went to as a young girl, whether to sew, read, play the piano, or ice skate. Today, I go to my office."

Do you have a place where you can go to dream, where you can bring forth who you are—and who you want to become?

ASKING FOR RESOURCES

In theory, clearing a space sounds easy. In reality, it's not. When we clear a space, we are moving aside something (probably something we're doing *for* someone else) to make space for *our* thing. And by extension, we're asking for resources, such as physical space, time, or money. Many of us have forgotten how to do this. Fortunately, young girls have not.

For instance, when my daughter Miranda was seven, she asked if we could go see *The Nutcracker* together. At that moment, she seemed to want more mother-daughter time, perhaps because she was feeling that my "work time" was displacing her "mom time." I wasn't surprised that Miranda suggested a girls' night out, but I was surprised by her ability to articulate so easily what she wanted. I'm not very good at stating what I want, and I don't know many women who are. Think about it: When was the last time a woman you know (or you yourself) asked simply and directly for something, and asked without any martyrdom, manipulation, etcetera? How often do women just declare what they want (without making it a need) and ask for it forcefully?

That's what I thought.

Our cultural ideals of femininity do not include women asking for resources, such as time, money, or even praise. When or if we do ask, we feel selfish, and it's quite likely we'll be looked at as being selfish.

During that Christmas there were many lovely gifts given and received in our home, but taking Miranda to see *The Nutcracker*, as my mother had once taken me, and hearing her ask for the outing without even a nanosecond's worry that she would be jeopardizing her femininity was, without a doubt, among the best gifts I received.

Janika Dillon, a mother of four who also holds a master's degree in organizational behavior, shares an incredible example of how she made space for herself.

Janika Dillon: *Taking a Staycation*

Since last October, our family has been planning a spring break trip to visit friends and historical sites in Pennsylvania, a trip for which I had:

1. Researched where to eat, what to see, entrance fees, best driving routes, and so on.
2. Made a neat pile of all my research and had a two-page packing and things-to-do list.
3. Gone to the library and checked out children's books and tapes about Gettysburg, Valley Forge, and more.
4. Selected travel-friendly activities for my children and bought lots of snacks.
5. Done the laundry, packed the bags, vacuumed the car, cleared out the fridge, and cleaned the entire house.

Are you tired yet? I was. Just moments before our planned departure, I realized that the last thing I wanted to do was take a week-long road trip. I told my husband, "You know, I really don't want to go on this trip. I just want to stay home all by myself for five days." It was like a wish come true: he quickly agreed, as did our four kids. Within minutes they were gone, without me.

I found myself suddenly alone in a perfectly clean and quiet house. I had no desire to venture out; I just wanted to luxuriate in time by myself. I made a long list of things I wanted to do.

I telephoned my eighty-eight-year-old grandparents and we had a delightful hour-long conversation. A few minutes later, a dear friend from high school called. We spoke for two hours, our friendship never missing a beat.

I began to sort through files on my desk, finding scribbled notes on tiny scraps of paper with phone numbers. In a life focused upon my husband and four children, I had left a wake of neglected friendships and missed opportunities. I had filled my mind with so many to-do lists in the midst of mothering chaos that I had forgotten how to hear my own voice. When a quiet moment did come, I didn't know how to use my free time because I didn't even know what I wanted to do.

With everyone gone, I thought I would feel lonely. I figured I would listen to books on tape all day to keep me company. But I wasn't lonely. I loved the silence and the opportunity to hear my thoughts, to wonder what I'd think up next, to wake up early, my mind spinning with so many new ideas.

One morning I woke up with a plan to improve my town's Patriots Day celebration. Each year, our town reenacts Paul Revere's ride, completing the event with a mini-parade, a speech from the mayor, a performance by the high school band, and lunch at a Revolutionary-era funeral home. My early-morning idea was to involve the city historical society, and the local university and other city and business organizations to sponsor several historical activity tables so children can learn more about Paul Revere and the history of our town.

It was refreshing to discover that I felt so strongly about something that I was willing to step outside of my comfort zone to make it happen. In my normal, nonrebellious, nonhermetic life, I often find myself pushing away really good ideas because I just don't have the time to develop or implement them. Maybe this time away from the noise would allow me to set some priorities for myself, enough at least to guide me until the next time I could take a "break."

American folklorist and mythologist Joseph Campbell wrote:

> You must have a room, or certain hour of the day or so, where you don't know what was in the newspapers that morning, you don't know who your friends are, you don't know what you owe anybody, you don't know what anybody owes to you. This is a place where you can experience and bring forth what you are and what you might be. This is the place of creative incubation. At first you may find that nothing happens there. But if you have a sacred place and use it, something eventually will happen.

As I carried on coherent conversations with my long-lost friends, many were at first shocked that I would stay home without my husband and children as I did. But then, after realizing what I had achieved, they'd enthusiastically say, "Oh, that's exactly what I want to do!"

I'm having a perfect staycation. I highly recommend you take one, as well.

Janika wisely recognized that she needed time and space to reconnect with herself in order to find her dreams, and she was brave enough to ask for the resources she needed. Kudos to her husband and children for giving her what she most needed!

In addition to making time and space to dream, some dreams may also require that we spend money. Most of us will sacrifice anything for our children's happiness, but asking for financial resources for our own dreams can feel as if we're asking for the moon. This is terribly difficult for me as well, which is probably one of the reasons I work to earn money. (If I make money, I don't have to ask for money.) So let's not think about asking for money. For now, let's just think about what it means when we spend money.

A DOWN PAYMENT ON OUR DREAMS

Consider for a moment Charles Dickens' assertion, "Annual income twenty pounds, annual expenditure nineteen and six, result happiness. Annual income twenty pounds, annual expenditure twenty pounds ought and six, result misery."

Spend less than we earn. I couldn't agree more. But once we've achieved this basic principle of money management, then what? How do we spend our money? Does how we spend mirror how we see the world? Do our spending habits enable our dreams?

When we spend money to house, feed, clothe, educate, and play with our children, aren't we making a down payment on their happiness, their identity, and ideally our shared desires to have a close-knit family? What about money spent on savings and investment? When we participate in philanthropic pursuits, aren't we casting a vote for a world where we take care of our own and others? There are so many great ways to spend our money. But, I wonder: Is there any room in our budget to finance our individual dreams?

As women, we may feel we don't have the money—or time or permission—to put toward our dream. But keep in mind that Psyche didn't need to shear the rams and obtain *all* the fleece. She needed only a little, a bit that the rams had snagged on the brambles. She could be heroic with just a little bit of fleece. You can too, with just a little bit of time, a little bit of money. Think of the money as a down payment on your dream.

If right about now you have that pit-in-the-stomach feeling

and you're thinking, "I can't possibly ask for time, or space, or money for myself," then consider morning sickness. One theory is that when a fetus starts to grow, a woman's body issues an "intruder" alert and launches an attack, just as it would with germs, viruses, even a transplanted organ. Morning sickness can be unendurable for a time. But when we finally cradle our newborn baby, those months of sickness seem a small price to pay. Making space for a new piece of ourselves may feel profoundly discomfiting, but isn't it also true that, once we give birth, we can become more ourselves than ever?

In the 1950s, Anne Morrow Lindbergh, the accomplished writer and poet, wrote in her acclaimed book *Gift from the Sea:*

> If women were convinced that a day off or an hour of solitude was a reasonable ambition, they would find a way of attaining it. As it is, they feel so unjustified in their demand that they rarely make the attempt. One has only to look at those women who actually have the economic means or the time and energy for solitude yet do not use it, to realize that the problem is not solely economic. It is more a question of inner convictions than of outer pressures, though, of course, the outer pressures are there and make it more difficult.... How inexplicable it seems. Anything else will be accepted as a better excuse. If one sets aside time for a business appointment, a trip to the hairdresser, a social engagement, that time is accepted as inviolable. But if one says: I cannot come because that is my hour to be alone, one is considered rude...and has to apologize for it.

Can you relate to what she's saying? Lindbergh continues, "When one is alone, it is among the most important times in one's life. Certain springs are tapped only when we are alone. The artist knows he must be alone to create; the writer, to work out his thoughts; the musician, to compose; the saint, to pray. Women need solitude to find again the true essence of themselves: that firm strand which will be the indispensable center of a whole web of human relationships."

When we make time, find space for, and invest in our dreams, we make an investment in the true essence of ourselves. On the surface, we may each be asking for what *we* want—but there will be a tremendous return on investment for our loved ones as well.

BRINGING FORTH WHAT YOU MIGHT BE...

Paraphrasing Joseph Campbell, you must claim a space and a time to discover what you are and who you might be.

- Why does making space for our dreams matter?
- Do you have a space set aside for dreaming? Physical space? A time of day?
- Why can practicing how to ask for what we want help us achieve our dreams?
- Do you know any women who ask for what they want? How do they ask and do they succeed in getting what they asked for?
- Have you taken a solo staycation? Did it help you move your dreams forward?

Every time you spend money, you're casting a vote for the kind of world you want.

—Anna Lappe, author and activist

- Do a quick review of the money you spend each month: How much is spent on your children's dreams? Your spouse's dreams? The dreams of your extended family, friends, the world? How much is spent on yours?

- How can we harness Charles Dickens' advice to make a down payment on our own dreams?

- If you do not currently generate paid income, are any funds in your household budget allocated to you? Are you comfortable with the arrangement you have?

To dare is to lose one's footing momentarily. To not dare is to lose oneself.
   —Søren Kierkegaard, nineteenth-century Danish philosopher

- As you think about making space for your dream, are you finding yourself uncomfortable, unnerved, even physically sick?

7

INVENTORY YOUR STRENGTHS
AND COMPETENCIES

W hat if one of your children came home from school with this report card:

Math: A
Geography: A+
Social Science: A
English: C
French: A

What would you think? What would you say?

During a presentation titled "Women at Their Best: Authentically Engaging Strengths for Maximal Contributions," Laura Morgan Roberts, PhD, the lead author on a *Harvard Business Review* paper titled "How to Play to Your Strengths," indicated that we will perfunctorily say "Good job" in math, geography, social science, and French but spend far more time trying to understand what caused the C in English and formulating a plan for improvement. "We will only see the C," she says.

Is this true for you? It certainly is for me. Of greater concern is that, according to researchers Barbara L. Frederickson and Marcial F. Losada in a 2005 paper titled "Positive Affect and the Complex Dynamics of Human Flourishing," for every negative thing we say, we need to say three positive things to offset or cancel out the negative; within a marriage (I suspect with our children as well), the ratio increases from 3:1 to 5:1.

PLAYING TO YOUR STRENGTHS

How can we dream, really making a difference for ourselves—in our families, communities, workplace, and the world—if all we acknowledge are our perceived deficits?

Dr. Roberts asserts that if we will play to our strengths, we *can* dream. Roberts believes we have four types of strengths, which she identifies as:

1. Our innate talents
2. The competencies we've developed
3. What we believe (our principles)
4. Our identities (gender, race, ethnicity, religion)

When we know what our strengths are, we have a better sense of self and self-confidence, and we are more likely to validate and encourage others. When we play to our strengths we'll become the hero of our story, and we'll encourage others be the hero of theirs.

So, let's take an inventory of our strengths, starting in this chapter with our innate talents and competencies. We'll discuss our principles and identities in subsequent chapters.

DISCOVERING YOUR INNATE TALENTS

Innate (adj.) existing in, belonging to, or determined by factors present in an individual from birth; NATIVE, INBORN

To discover our innate talents, we can ask ourselves some questions:

1. What did you like to do as a little girl and why?
2. What are your intelligences?
3. What makes you feel strong?

REMEMBERING CHILDHOOD

As a young girl, I loved to play the piano and I especially loved to ice skate. My sense of self surged as I glided over the ice. On the drive to the rink we often listened to Helen Reddy belt "I Am Woman" on our eight-track player. (Seems my desire to affirm "us girls" started at the tender age of ten.) I also loved to ski and to play dodgeball. With the latter, I prided myself on being one of the first girls picked and on often being picked before several of the boys. I played to win and I had many a sprained finger to prove it.

Reading was another childhood love. My sister and I frequently spent Saturday afternoons racing through Nancy Drew books while lounging on our bunk beds in our house on Dumbarton Avenue. Books continue to be beloved friends, and my daughter often asks why I scribble in the margins.

I also enjoyed sewing. My mother would take my sister and me to San Jose's Pruneyard Mall to buy patterns and fabric. I'd rush home from fourth and fifth grade so I could construct a new dress, ice skating outfit, or nightgown. What a sense of satisfaction I felt when I wore something I had made! My very first dress was a sailor dress: blue denim kettle cloth with a white collar and a red ribbon, tied sailor style. I wore it on the first day of fourth grade.

As I reflect on my childhood loves, I can uncover my innate talents, especially when I look behind *what* I was doing, to the reason *why* I loved doing it. My sense of self, and my ability to succeed at what I did were important and emerged as I practiced the piano, ice skated, skied, played dodge ball, and read Nancy Drew.

As children, we did what we loved to do. When we examine what we loved to do when we were young, we are likely to discover or rediscover our innate talents. As adults we may no longer do the things we loved as children. For example, I no longer sew or ice skate. Yet the whys behind what I do as an adult are startlingly similar to the whys of my childhood passions. Furthermore, when we find we are really enjoying something, luxuriating in what we are doing, we're likely drawing from the well of our native talents. This is precisely what happened with Mary Alice Hatch—she knew she loved to create as a child, which led to her dream as an adult to start her own interior design firm.

Mary Alice Hatch: *Creating Something Beautiful*

Since I was a small child, I have always loved to create. I love to create something magnificent from something ordinary. I love entering a new space and coming up with new possibilities.

As a young girl I constantly created new room layouts; when my parents would go on a trip I would repaint my furniture and add new hardware. In college, I started to build furniture; I also love to arrange flowers.

Because I have always enjoyed design, I went back to school

six years ago, taking a correspondence course in interior design from a school in New York City. Though I opened my own design studio in May of 2003, for the last three years, I've been my own client as I rebuilt an old boathouse and guesthouse at our home in New Hampshire.

In early 2008, *Architectural Digest* held an open submission, its first such contest. One of my lifelong goals has been to submit my work to a first-rate interior design publication like *Architectural Digest*. I knew the chance to be picked for the single published spot was slim, but I nonetheless photographed and submitted my boathouse, went to New York, and stood in line outside the Decoration and Design Building, New York's premiere design center.

When my time came to meet with one of the editors, I was so excited. As I showed the editor my "before" and "after" portfolio and listened to her expressions of interest, I had such a feeling of accomplishment. And when she asked if she could keep it to show Paige Reese, the editor-in-chief of the magazine, of course I said yes, and then floated out of the meeting. It was so validating to have someone at the top of my field like my project. I didn't win, but I was competitive—and that felt good, really good.

As we consider what we delighted in doing as children, there will undoubtedly be clues to our innate talents and dreams. If we aren't quite sure what these gifts are, it may just be time to revisit the playground that was our childhood.

PINPOINTING YOUR UNIQUE INTELLIGENCES

Another way of getting at our innate talents is to revisit the concept of intelligence. Is there only one kind of intelligence or are there multiple intelligences? Nineteenth-century novelist

Marcel Proust said that, "The real voyage of discovery lies not in seeking new landscapes but in seeing with new eyes."

A few years ago I was in a work-related continuing education course when the instructor commented, "You're really good at math." I remember thinking, "Really? Could he be right? Could it be true that I'm good at math?" I can pinpoint the moment I started to believe I was bad at math. This script, so to speak, began in fifth grade, when math involved word problems. In sixth grade, when my teacher told me to stop asking questions and just figure the question out on my own, and I thought I couldn't, I finalized the script. It read: "I'm bad at math."

The "I'm bad at math" script wouldn't be so problematic except that girls and women in the United States have a tendency to believe they *are* bad at math. Comparatively, boys and men don't appear to be as intimidated by math. Meanwhile, we live in a society whose systems and social structures value math skills. The script was problematic for me, specifically, because it isn't true.

Now, for the sake of argument, let's say that it was true that I have always and will forever struggle with math. Would that mean I'm dumb? No, because there isn't a single intelligence that we either have more or less of. There are instead multiple intelligences, Howard Gardner asserts, which include not only linguistic and logical-mathematical, but also musical, spatial, kinesthetic, naturalist, interpersonal, intrapersonal, and existential.

Linguistic intelligence means being adept in written and spoken language. Mathematical intelligence involves the ability to calculate numbers. These are the two intelligences measured by most schools and standardized tests. If you've gone through school and even some of your work life feeling dumb (as I often have) because you weren't particularly strong linguistically or mathematically, it's time to look at yourself with new eyes. It's time you recognize just how smart and capable and competent you are.

Here are some other ways people are smart:

Musical intelligence: Do you play an instrument, sing well, or compose music? Are you adept at organizing a conference or event, producing a play, or giving a speech? All of these have their origin in musical structure."

Spatial intelligence: Are you comfortable with architecture, interior or landscape design, and organizing physical or cyber-space? Do you design tools, furniture, or toys?

Bodily-kinesthetic intelligence: Do you create products using your whole body or parts of your body, such as your hands? Do you paint, build furniture, scrapbook, sew, dance, play tennis?

Naturalist intelligence: Can you identify different plants and insects? Anyone involved in the preparation of food, construction of dwellings, or protection of the environment draws on her naturalist capacity.

Interpersonal intelligence: Can you look outward, toward the behavior and feelings of others, figuring out their motivations and working effectively with them? Are you able to understand what children or your colleagues want and broker win-win situations?

Intrapersonal intelligence: Can you identify your personal feelings, goals, fears, strengths, and weaknesses? As you examine your life and make changes, are you happier today than you were five years ago?

Existential intelligence: Can you pose and ponder the biggest questions: Who am I? What is the purpose of my life? What am I meant to do? Can I become the hero of my story? Many of the world's greatest leaders, such as Mahatma Gandhi and Winston

Churchill, have addressed these questions, helping us to make meaning of life's experiences in uplifting, redemptive ways. Filmmakers tackle these big questions, too. *Star Wars* is a good example. Existentialism is the intelligence we need in order to dream and figure out who we are so we can understand what we're meant to do.

Is it really possible to see ourselves, our minds, with new eyes? I believe it is. Here's just one example. While organizing my home (under the direction of my friend, who possesses spatial intelligence) I found a media-training videotape of myself. When I first saw the tape six years ago I perceived myself as being dumb, tongue-tied, and fat. Everything I saw was negative. With time, I'm seeing with new eyes, and in watching the tape I'm finding aspects of myself to be proud of.

We may not always be intelligent in the traditional, academically testable sense of intelligence, but each of us *is* intelligent. Our particular brand of intelligence is part of our portfolio of strengths. When you ponder this list of intelligences and have that *aha!* moment—and you will—you'll be another step closer to piecing together your dream.

CLUEING IN TO WHAT MAKES YOU FEEL STRONG

Marcus Buckingham, a former researcher for the Gallup Organization who has studied what drives performance and coauthor of *Now, Discover Your Strengths,* wrote:

> Our strengths can be so easy to overlook, because they clamor for attention in the most basic way: Using them makes you feel strong. All you have to do is teach yourself to

pay attention. Most of the time, we're so focused on getting our work done that we don't really have time to notice how we feel about it. But when you make the conscious effort to notice yourself at work (or at play, for that matter), you will find that you experience what I call "strong-moments" throughout your day—times when you feel invigorated, inquisitive, successful. Those moments are the best clues as to what your strengths are.

The simple acronym SIGN, developed by Buckingham, can help you recognize your signs of strength:

S Success: Do you feel a sense of accomplishment about finishing this task?

I Instinct: Do you instinctively look forward to this task?

G Growth: Are your synapses firing? Are you mentally focused?

N Needs: Does this task fulfill one of your needs?

Acknowledging our "strong-moments" and identifying the talents that are evidenced when we feel invigorated, inquisitive, and successful will help us not only find our dreams but have the confidence to pursue them.

RECOGNIZING YOUR SKILLS

Another place we can look to identify our strengths and gain clues to our dreams is in our competencies.

In contrast to our innate talents, our competencies are skills that we've developed because we do something frequently, perhaps purposefully, perhaps not. This may be in the course of our daily lives. We are good at getting up at 6:00 A.M. because we do this every day and have for twenty years. Perhaps we set out to be early risers, perhaps our work (as mothers and/or in the paid workforce) has required that we wake before dawn. Another wellspring of competencies can be found in the challenges and daunting tasks we didn't choose. We become competent because we faced the challenge, walked through the fear, and developed strengths we had no idea we could or would.

Let's start with things we do habitually, such as parenting. When the first child is born, most of us have no idea what we're doing. We eventually learn to parent well because we jump in and sink or swim. Though we may feel like we're sinking at times, most of us are able to keep our children safe, serving as models for how to be good people and contributing members of society. Parenting is a competency we develop over time and it encompasses many skills that we can apply to pursuing our dreams.

MINING FOR COMPETENCIES

A competency I've developed is speaking Spanish. I studied Spanish in school and lived in Uruguay for more than a year as a missionary. I've had further opportunities to practice because much of my professional life has centered on Latin America. Because I've learned Spanish, I am better able to walk in the figurative shoes of another culture, and I have fondness and respect for people I meet from both Spain and Latin America. I know what it's like to have to translate ideas from one language to another. Translating (both figuratively and literally from one language to another) is a skill I use often in business and in the interfaith work I have done. Perhaps most importantly, learning to find my voice in Spanish has helped me find my voice in English. In Spanish, I speak more plainly, more boldly, and without apology, far more than I do in English.

Another ability I have is to analyze a company and build a financial model to determine whether a company is creating or destroying value. I'm also very skilled at crafting an investment thesis. Initially, I wasn't good at either—just ask my first boss in equity research. Trying and not succeeding was painful, but I stayed with it and I became good at the work. Having built many a financial model and written hundreds of research reports, I now know what I'm doing when I analyze an investment.

Sometimes we set out to become competent. At other times our competence is simply an unintended consequence of doing what needs to be done, as was the case for Amy Jo Schenewark. In the summer of 2009 she packed up her children and temporarily relocated from Ohio to New Hampshire to care for her younger sister Becky and Becky's family, while she was bedridden due to a difficult pregnancy and subsequent surgery.

Amy Jo Schenewark: *On Giving Care*

I remember listening to NPR one evening in 2007 while Lee Woodruff, the wife of TV journalist Bob Woodruff, talked about caring for her husband after he sustained a traumatic brain injury while reporting for ABC News in Iraq. I thought, "Wow. I'm glad I'm not there. I don't know how people do it." I remember my mother taking care of her father. It began with weekly checks on him at his house, then involved moving him into her house and finally to a care facility. I know she gave him all her spare time, thoughts, and energy.

When Lee Woodruff took questions from caregivers who called in to the broadcast, I could sense the immediate connection between her and the callers. These strangers became instant friends because they understood the burden they all carry: the unrelenting, never-ending, sometimes frustrating, often draining, and physically exhausting service to a family member.

When I became a necessary caregiver in the summer of 2009, I remembered those thoughts, but I tucked them away in a safe place because I knew they could overwhelm me. I labored for my sister, for her children, for my children, for her handicapped child—and, via long distance, for my husband. I cooked and cleaned as usual, it was just for more people. I gardened. I gathered medicines and supplies, learned about machines and equipment, signed for and unpacked medical supply deliveries, made mistakes, learned how to stay ahead of the curve. I suctioned, hooked up G-tubes, put in a catheter, mixed feeding bags, administered medication.

One day I was in the grocery store, waiting for my items to be scanned, when an item set off a beep that sounded just like a medical alarm back at the house. It scared me because I thought Ben was having oxygen issues or that Becky's IV bag was empty. I relaxed once I remembered where I was.

My two months as a caregiver seemed liked a lifetime. I forgot what my house looked like, who my friends were, what my husband smelled like. And it made me wonder:

- How do caregivers keep going?
- Who supports them when they want or need a break?
- How do they deal with emotional drains?
- How do they fulfill their own dreams?
- How long should they put their dreams on the back burner?
- Are they too tired to have dreams?

Caring for Becky and her family was fulfilling because I care deeply about her and I was succeeding at something I never dreamed I was capable of doing. But the work was never ending, and even though I didn't have to do the nights, I had no down time. I also knew that, for me, the situation was temporary; it was two months of my time. It helped me understand the life of a caregiver and gave me a fresh perspective on my own life.

Full-time caregiving was not Amy's first choice (and she already had six boys of her own to care for), but she got good at what needed to be done and in the process developed a great compassion and appreciation for those who are full-time caregivers.

OVERCOMING CHALLENGES

The opportunity to develop competencies may be handed to us in the form of a crisis, as was the case with Brooksley Born, the first female president of the Law Review at Stanford, the first female to finish at the top of the class and an expert in commodities and futures. Charged with the oversight of the U.S. government's Commodity Futures Trading Commission (CFTC) by the Clinton Administration, Born could foresee what would happen if there wasn't more regulatory oversight in the multitrillion dollar derivatives markets. Yet no one in government or in the financial markets would listen; in 2008 alone, the U.S. market lost about $8 trillion in value. She has since been dubbed the "Credit Crisis Cassandra." In Greek mythology, Cassandra was given both the gift of seeing the future and the curse of having no one believe her predictions.

In the case of Brooksley Born, the attacks by very powerful

people were harsh and unrelenting. She was right, while those around her were gravely wrong. Yet, when I listen to Born and read her interviews, there is no anger, no recrimination in her voice, only grace. Brooksley Born never would have chosen this situation. She recounts waking in a cold sweat many a night. She has learned from her trial by fire and we can learn from her.

Sometimes we set out to develop competencies, sometimes we don't. Either way, if we do something enough, we are likely to get good at it. As poet Emily Dickinson wrote,

> *Luck is not chance—*
> *It's toil—*
> *Fortune's expensive smile*
> *Is earned.*

PUTTING IN THE WORK

In his 2008 book, *Outliers*, Malcolm Gladwell outlines "the 10,000-hour rule." He writes, "For almost a generation, psychologists around the world have been engaged in a spirited debate over a question most of us would consider to have been settled years ago. The question is this: is there such a thing as innate talent? The obvious answer is yes. Not every child that plays the piano grows up to be a concert pianist."

Gladwell does, however, put a dent in the innate talent theory, citing a study indicating that elite performers have totaled ten thousand hours of practice by age twenty, the good students about eight thousand hours, and the future music teachers about four thousand hours. Once a musician has enough ability to get into a top music school, what distinguishes one performer from another is determined by how hard he or she works. That's it. What's more, the people at the very top don't just work harder or even *much* harder than everyone else, they work much, *much* harder. Gladwell further supports his view, quoting Daniel Levitin, a musician-turned-neurologist and author of *This Is Your Brain on Music.* "The emerging picture from such studies is that ten thousand hours of practice is required to achieve the level of mastery associated with being a world-class expert—in anything," says Levitin. While talent does matter, the opportunity to consistently practice matters more.

These findings are heartening to those of us who dream. You and I will ultimately dream of doing something that builds on our innate talents and strengths because it invigorates us—it is our gift. By cataloguing what we loved to do as children, by examining personal intelligences, what we enjoy doing today, and what makes us feel strong, we will be well on our way to identifying our strengths. We develop competencies, expertise that comes quite often as we face our most vexing challenges. These competencies are strengths and are important tools in shaping and achieving our dreams. Finally, we need to have opportunities, namely resources, available in order to pursue our dreams. We can get good at what we care about. We simply need the opportunity to practice.

IDENTIFYING YOUR INNATE TALENTS AND COMPETENCIES . . .

- How will recognizing your strengths help you dream?
- Are there clues as to your innate talents either in what you loved to do as a child or why you loved to do it?

Too many people overvalue what they are not and undervalue what they are.

> —Malcolm Forbes, publisher

- After reading about multiple intelligences, what intelligence do you have that you didn't previously recognize?

The foolish man seeks happiness in the distance, the wise just under his feet.

> —James Oppenheim, American poet

- If you were to write down for a week what you enjoyed doing each day, not what you think you should enjoy, what would be on your list?
- What kinds of projects or undertakings do you find yourself salivating over?

What if everything you think is wrong with you is really a superpower?

> —Liz Strauss, social media strategist

- What things have you become good at because of challenges you faced?
- Are dreams emerging from these competencies?

8

KNOW YOUR DEEPLY
HELD BELIEFS

We have already established that identifying our strengths is key to defining our dreams. In the preceding chapters we discussed innate talents and acquired competencies. The third category of strengths is our principles, including the core religious beliefs by which we define ourselves. Whether we come from a strong religious tradition or not, we all have a basic foundation of principles and beliefs that guide our actions and are an essential part of our truest selves. Identifying these foundational ideas can help us uncover and delineate our deepest dreams.

About six months after my husband and I moved to New York City, I was waiting for the train at Lincoln Center and animatedly describing a film I had seen at Lincoln Center a few days before to a group of women from my church. I was excited to be living in New York, discovering, seeing, learning—and I was happy. After a few minutes of listening to my enthusiastic description of the film, a woman a few years younger than me, whose husband was in school and who had two children, declared dismissively, "You really do need to start having children."

Pop went my bubble.

It's been twenty years, but I still remember the who, what, where, and when of that encounter. I was hurt. To be fair, I know I've said similarly hurtful and judgmental things to other women. But the comment, coming from someone with whom I shared a religious tradition, led me to wonder: Was I bad because I didn't yet have children? Because I had time and money to go see a movie? Was it wrong of me to be pursuing a career? Within my church culture, there is an expectation that a woman's first priority is to have children; a career is not considered as important or as desirable as motherhood, and there's a perception that career and motherhood don't mix.

These were questions I needed to grapple with. They were among the "big questions" I needed to ask and answer. At the time, the answer for us was that pursuing our careers and delaying parenthood was the right decision. It was also an imperative for me, in part because of my religious tradition, to eventually become a mother. Yet I faced the reality of needing to earn money while my husband was in school. Furthermore, I *wanted* to work and have a career. I knew these incongruities needed to be reconciled.

Ten years later, I faced another tough decision. I was now a new, first-time mom. I had moved from investment banking to equity research and my husband was busy with his post-doctoral fellowship and responsibilities at church. On top of that, I was about halfway through grad school at New York University. This time around, the answer was family first. I dropped out of NYU. Occasionally I still pine for the master's in business administration I don't have, but at that moment stepping away was the right choice.

DREAMING INSPIRED BY CORE BELIEFS

Our deeply held beliefs can put boundaries on our dreams, but as our dreams tap into what we hold most dear, these same principles provide scaffolding for our emerging dreams. Neylan McBaine, a Yale University graduate, and the founder and editor of The Mormon Women Project (mormonwoman.com), is an example of how our dreams are inspired by and spring from our deeply held beliefs.

Neylan McBaine: *The Mormon Women Project*

I'm a born-and-raised New Yorker: a Manhattanite, at that. I went to one of those Gossip Girl schools, the one Jackie Kennedy attended as a girl. I am the daughter of an opera singer and a lawyer, and that makes me a bohemian with a Wall Street sensibility. My educational pedigree continued at the Julliard School, where I studied piano, and Yale University, where I majored in English.

But there is one label that defines me more than all of these fancy designations: I am a Mormon. Not just any Mormon, a Mormon woman, which means that people I meet, when assaulted with all the brand names and movie-set locations of my childhood, get a very confused look on their face when they also find out I go to church for three hours a week, sustain a living prophet, and believe the *Book of Mormon* to be the word of God. "But aren't you a thinking person?" their look seems to ask. Or, as one of my dearest New York friends revealed one tipsy evening, "How did I become friends with a freakin' Mormon?"

If left merely to the impressions of the media, one might understandably think that a woman with my background couldn't possibly be affiliated with an organization that—as it is so often presented—funnels its women into wifely and motherly servitude and has some sort of relationship (no one's quite sure) with polygamy. But Mormonism's best-kept secret is that intelligent, engaged, and proactive women are legion in our culture. Why doesn't anyone know about us?

Part of the problem is that many Mormon women themselves don't recognize that these intelligent, engaged women are in our midst. Many are afraid to admit they are one of these women. "If I were a 'good' Mormon, I wouldn't have gotten my master's degree. I wouldn't be working, and I wouldn't want to work so much. I'd want to be a mother and have kids and stay home," one young filmmaker said to me. How did we get to a point in our culture where our free agency—the ability to choose, which our doctrine holds as the most ennobled quality of our human condition—has been disparaged to the degree that a young, talented woman feels ashamed of her pursuits?

The importance of marriage and motherhood is never in question among faithful Mormons, and my own youth was filled with female role models who remain true to themselves, their talents, their interests, and their families. With the help of prayer, faith, and a hard-won understanding of our unique missions in life, this balance is not only possible, it is demanded by a doctrine that celebrates individual worth. But this balance is not widely practiced. As I've grown older, I've seen many Mormon women feel ostracized and sometimes leave the church altogether because they're not sure how their choices fit into "the mold." These experiences have prompted me to share some of the role models from my own life and search out others who have made thoughtful, considered choices about who they want to be.

I founded The Mormon Women Project to shed light on the immense strength and variety of the seven million

Mormon women throughout the world. The project, housed at mormonwomen.com, is a digital library of interviews with Latter-Day Saint women. My hope is that by profiling women who have made proactive choices in their lives, while still remaining committed to their faith, the project will broaden the definition of what it means to be a Mormon woman today.

Faustina Otoo, a convert to the church in Accra, Ghana, is just as "Mormon" as a young, full-time mother in Utah.

So, too, is Myrna Castellar, a recovering heroin addict in New York.

Karen Bybee is no less a mother to her three sons because she has a successful international sports management career planning World Cup and Olympic events.

With single women making up the largest single demographic of church membership, student Jenny Reeder should be lauded for her pursuit of a doctorate, not left out because she hasn't yet married.

The power of our stories comes from the irony inherent in their telling: at once, we feel the commonness and also the uniqueness of our own personal circumstance. Our faith in a common doctrine brings us together as a people, despite our varying locales or ages or ethnicities. Yet each of our stories is so individual that we cannot doubt the power of our personal missions and the solitary responsibility we each have to make something of ourselves.

Neylan's dreams have been sculpted by her religious identity, and her quest to help Mormon women see the diversity in their ranks is inspired by dearly held beliefs instilled by her parents, her church, and her particular upbringing in New York City. My dream to be a missionary for a year and a half during my early twenties sprang from my belief in God. Like Abigail

Adams, I believed and continue to believe that, "religion is the only sure and permanent foundation of life." Madeleine L'Engle, the beloved children's author, echoes the sentiment. About her Newbery Award–winning book *A Wrinkle in Time*, she wrote, "If I've ever written a book that says what I feel about God and the universe this is it. This is my psalm of praise."

What we believe propels each of us uniquely. Contrast L'Engle's experience of writing a psalm of praise with the experience of Ranya Idliby. Idliby is an American Muslim of Palestinian descent. She is the coauthor of *The Faith Club*, a book written by mothers of three different faiths about their experience in the aftermath of September 11th. Idliby writes, "As the city began to mourn, churches and temples opened their doors for worship and emotional support. I longed for a mosque or a Muslim religious leader who could help support my family during this horrific time. I needed a spiritual community, a safe haven where we could seek comfort." In a time of tragedy, Idliby sought comfort in her faith.

This was an especially difficult time to be a Muslim in American, as Idliby was both challenged by those of her faith ("Muslims abroad who questioned the possibility of a future for American Muslims") and those not of her faith ("the stereotypes and prejudices were heightened by 9/11"), and she again looked to her core religious beliefs for answers. She writes, "As I started researching Islam, I stumbled upon Muhammad's night flight journey and ascension to heaven in which Muhammad rides a magical winged horse ridden before him by Jesus, Moses, and other biblical prophets. As he ascends a jeweled staircase to the kingdom of God, Muhammad is welcomed by various prophets as a fellow brother and prophet."

This *canonized* story prompted the thought, "Wouldn't it be wonderful to find a Christian and a Jewish mother to write a children's book with me that would highlight the connection within Judaism, Christianity, and Islam?" The result of her conversations with Suzanne Oliver and Priscilla Warner wasn't ultimately as simple as a children's book, but rather a memoir of spiritual reflection titled *The Faith Club*: *A Muslim, a Christian, a Jew—Three Women Search for Understanding.* Idliby's deeply held beliefs not only provided solace to her, but her beliefs became the driver of a dream.

Even when we aren't sure we want to espouse our deeply ingrained beliefs, they are there and they influence what we do. Penelope Trunk, the founder of *Brazen Careerist*, a blog/social network to help young people manage their careers, writes:

> I am starting to think that the most effective preparation for a good career is religion.
>
> I am writing this post on the eve of Yom Kippur. I am constantly trying to figure out how religion fits in my life. Sometimes I think it doesn't fit. And I can't figure out what to do with my kids on Yom Kippur, so I'm sending them to school. I never once, in eighteen years, went to school on Yom Kippur. So I know it's going to feel [bad].
>
> I wish I could not care about religion because I'm an intellectual or because I'm fine doing it however I do it. But one thing that I know for sure is that religion is great preparation for getting what you want out of your work life...So while I'm being a bad Jew on Yom Kippur, I'm thinking that all career questions are really: "What is my purpose in life?"

When we dream within the context of what we believe—in effect asking and answering the question "What is my purpose in life?"—we believe that what we do really matters. And dreams that truly matter emerge from the deepest questions about who we are and what our lives should be.

DREAMING IN THE CONTEXT OF YOUR BELIEFS

It's not always easy to integrate our secular lives with our spiritual lives, which revolve around our principles, perhaps even our religion. Haven't we all had moments when we wish we could just ignore this piece of ourselves? But what we believe *is* who we are. There are unique tensions because of what we believe, but from these principles also come our strengths.

To close this chapter, I'd like to share some of my core beliefs, or guiding principles, that lead me to believe that dreaming is essential, help me sift through possible dreams, and encourage me as I seek to achieve my dreams.

> *You can bet your life, and that, and twice its double, that God knew exactly where he wanted you to be placed.*
>
> —Stevie Wonder, songwriter/musician

These lyrics, from Stevie Wonder's album *Songs in the Key of Life,* encapsulate what I believe about your life and mine. Each of us is exactly where we are supposed to be. So we can learn what we need to learn, accomplish what we are meant to accomplish, help those we were meant to help. In short, where we are, who we are, and what we do matters.

> *The only safe harbor is our convictions.*
>
> —Whitney Johnson (me!)

As I mentioned in chapter 2, I came by this principle or maxim the hard way. It was my job as an investment analyst to have an opinion about whether people should buy or sell certain stocks. Yet, I had grown up, as do most girls, learning to give up resources, including my views and opinions. This background made it difficult for me to expressly and publicly state my views because they would inevitably make someone angry with me. The experience taught me that I need to speak my truth, clearly and gently, and then let things fall where they may.

To be happy at home is the ultimate result of all ambition.
　　　—Samuel Johnson, eighteenth-century English author

This wisdom from Samuel Johnson is as true today as it was in the eighteenth century. If my dreams don't ultimately strengthen my relationships, if the fleece I gather isn't spun into wool that binds me to those I love, then it's not a dream I want to dream.

The desire to create is one of the deepest yearnings of the human soul.
　　—Dieter F. Uchtdorf, religious leader and former German aviator

When we create, we are dreaming and we are happy. Easier said than done. Hence, this book.

I pass the test.
　　　—Lady Galadriel in *Lord of the Rings*, J.R.R. Tolkien

When Frodo, encouraged by Lady Galadriel's goodness and wisdom, offers her the Ring, she wants to accept it, desperately.

She says, "I do not deny that my heart has greatly desired to ask what you offer. And now at last it comes. . . . I shall be beautiful and terrible as the Morning and the Night, stronger than the foundations of the earth. All shall love me and despair." No matter how much I may desire to do good, once I have that power, it can corrupt me. I want to "pass the test," as Galadriel did.

> *Coincidence is God's way of remaining anonymous.*
> —Albert Einstein, twentieth-century theoretical
> physicist and philosopher

Just as you and I choose whether to see coincidence or God's imprint in our lives, we choose to see doors to our dreams closing or opening.

> *Rings and other jewels are not gifts, but apologies for gifts. The only gift is a portion of thyself. . . Therefore the poet brings his poem; the shepherd, his lamb; the farmer, corn . . . the girl, a handkerchief of her own sewing . . . it is a cold, lifeless business when you go to the shops to buy me something, which does not represent your life and talent, but a goldsmith's.*
> —Ralph Waldo Emerson, nineteenth-century
> essayist and philosopher

Ralph Waldo Emerson says in one paragraph what it took me three chapters to say about our strengths. When we can uncover our strengths, or what I sometimes refer to as our magic, and share this with others, we give a true gift. For me, when I can help someone discover the gift she has to give, the achievement I feel is sublime.

*And thine ears shall hear a word behind thee saying, this is the
way, walk ye in it.*

—King James Bible, Isaiah 30:21

I saved this one for last because, for me, it's foundational to
dreaming. It's about believing that dreams are essential, that we
can discover our dreams and have the courage to pursue them.
Trust yourself. Trust your intuition, for God, I believe, is the
author of our intuition.

What we believe deeply inspires and informs our dreams,
creating unique tensions and opportunities, but only when
we dream within the context of our deeply held beliefs can we
discover what we were meant to do. As we articulate our core
beliefs, we will undoubtedly find that our dreams spring from
and are aligned with our cherished beliefs.

DRAWING ON DEEPLY HELD BELIEFS...

- If we want to have happy lives, we need to know the purpose of our lives. Doesn't dreaming involve figuring out
the purpose of our lives and having the resolve to accomplish that purpose?
- How does your core belief system, whether it's your faith or
otherwise, inform your choices and your dreams?
- What are your guiding principles?

9

BUILD ON YOUR FEMININE STRENGTHS

The fourth element of identifying our strengths is to look at identity—including our gender, race, religion, and ethnicity—and examine how these aspects of who we are can influence our dreams. In the prior chapter, we discussed how our principles, values, and religious beliefs are strengths. In this chapter we'll explore how being female is a truly great strength and what a tremendous impact our gender identity has on the direction of our dreams.

The Old Testament tells the story of Abigail and with her husband, Nabal, who were King David's subjects. (By the way, King David is the David who slew Goliath.) The Bible describes Nabal as "churlish and evil in his doings." When approached by King David's servants for provisions, Nabal refuses. An incensed King David vows to kill him. To save her husband's life, Abigail "gathers two hundred loaves, two bottles of wine, five sheep ready dressed, and five measures of corn, a hundred clusters of raisins, and two hundred cakes of figs." She prostrates herself before the king, begs for forgiveness, and pleads for Nabal's crime to be on her head.

King David forgives Abigail, saying "Go up in peace to thine house...I have hearkened to thy voice, and accepted thy person." The importance of the story is not David's mercy but Abigail's bravery—and her strength. Abigail was willing to sacrifice her life for her boorish, foolish husband. The feminine willingness to give everything, perhaps even our lives, for those we love is a strength, as is tenderness toward those who may not be deserving of our love.

In mythology we see this strength in Psyche, who is willing to undertake four Herculean tasks, including literally going through hell to be reunited with Eros (aka Cupid). As women, we tend to be driven by love, and our innate desires for marriage, children, and nurturing happy relationships exert a powerful influence on our dreams. We see evidence of this in the story shared on *Dare to Dream* by my friend Jane Clayson Johnson. As an anchor for CBS's *The Early Show*, Jane met a grandmother in Shantou, China, who, seeing a newborn abandoned because she had a cleft palate, scooped up the child and vowed to care for her.

Perhaps this is why so many of us are drawn to the idea of microcredit, the financial lending system in which small loans, made primarily to women in third world nations, provide funds that change lives. When we meet women (like those I met in Uruguay) who have been dealt a tough hand yet are ferociously doing whatever needs to be done to feed and clothe their children, we instinctively relate to them. We understand why they are doing what they are doing, and we understand their willingness to sacrifice for those they love. Closer to home, I watch mothers who, day in and day out, feed and clothe their children and remind them to do their homework, practice the piano, do their chores, and be kind to their siblings. Mothers rarely give up. Yes, there are the occasional rants. If we weren't connected to our loved ones, we probably wouldn't bother, but mostly there is tenderness.

What many women do on a daily basis, the efforts we make on behalf of others, deserves praise and accolades. There is no guarantee of a reward for our nurturing. To the extent we are rewarded, it is usually deferred, sometimes for decades. We often do what we do without credit and for long periods of time because it needs to be done. This is a feminine strength, one that serves us well when we dream of being a mother, as has Julia Blake.

Julia Blake: *Living My Dream*

I'm not sure I should blame *Dare to Dream* for distracting me from my dream. In nineteen years of marriage and seventeen years of motherhood, distraction has been the norm. I was a pre-med major and sometimes regret not going to medical school. I have often looked around at mothers who are businesswomen, doctors, investors, artists, architects, and writers and dreamed of being like them. Since having children I have started successful businesses, managed record-breaking fundraisers, had products featured in *Boston Baby* magazine, renovated homes, and much more, all while being a "stay-at-home-mom." Yet none of these were my primary dream.

When I encountered *Dare to Dream* I was erroneously convinced that I was falling short of my potential if I didn't pursue some big dream outside of motherhood. Eventually, I pushed back at this distortion to recognize that I am living my dream and that I do not want lesser dreams to overpower it. My dream is to *enjoy* a successful marriage and family.

I didn't achieve my dream when I got married and had children—it had just begun. I was a different person the moment my first child was placed on my chest in the delivery room. I felt my life take on a significance that it didn't have previously. It is not always joyful—many times during those early years, I felt I was in way over my head and clawing just to make it through each day. Today it still isn't joy when ungrateful kids ignore what I have taught them, pass bad habits along to younger siblings, fight with each other, and let their gym clothes fester in the locker room all year. The sheer quantity of what is required of me overwhelms at times. I try to laugh at the reality that I can't finish the laundry, clean the house, provide nutritious meals, exercise, and shower all in the same week.

This past fall I realized that I had comically overcommitted myself, yet I comprehended that this was my time to be involved. I knew that my deepest satisfaction was in doing the work that accompanies raising children. For example, it makes me blissful to feed my teenage boys. They sincerely appreciate my food. When I sign up to feed the football team, I'm not having it catered and I am not cutting corners. I'm making a complete dinner from scratch. My boys see that I put the time in for them and their friends. Admittedly, I love hearing that ours was the best team dinner. That's more than enough payment for me. All of the homemaking tasks are the collateral to my dream and not what actually matters, except to the extent that they bring happiness. If I can be happy doing the tasks and involve my children in them, then the work is an important part of the goal.

I love waking up in the morning and deciding what I want to do. I don't have a boss or a client dictating that. If I don't feel like doing the laundry, the kids can do it themselves or wear something else. If I don't clean the house, I am the only one who cares. When I skip the grocery shopping or don't cook, we eat cereal. I love being able to choose.

I get to go to my kids' sports events, help them practice the piano, tutor them academically, play games with them, read to them, listen to them, teach them to scrub a toilet and hang up their clothes, stay awake with them when they are sick, and so on. Of course, there are parts of my job that I like better than others. Above all, I recognize that I have the freedom every day to choose how I want to improve, who I want to serve, and what I want to create and accomplish. By some blessed chance I have come to a place where I don't feel guilt for what I do and don't do. When I take a few hours or days for myself and personal interests I don't feel the guilt that I once did. Maybe it is because I decided that this dream is enough.

In less than two years my oldest will leave home. I am clinging to every day I have with him. When my youngest is gone I will evaluate new dreams, but for now this one requires everything I have.

Whether we mother our own children or—as aunts, teachers, community leaders, or neighbors—we mother someone else's children, feminine strengths of being indefatigable, fearless, and gentle are vital to the health and well-being of our communities and our families and even to the survival of the human race. Mothering, in all its forms, springs from our feminine nature, and, while not universal, it is a widespread and important dream for many women.

NURTURING YOURSELF

One of the risks of the motherhood dream is that no one knows exactly what we do—and frankly, sometimes neither do we. Michael Lewis, the author of *The Blind Side*, wrote about professional basketball player Shane Battier, who plays for the Houston

Rockets, in an article titled "The No-Stats All-Star." He describes Battier as follows: "Shane Battier is widely regarded inside the NBA as, at best, a replaceable cog in a machine driven by superstars. And yet every team he has ever played on has acquired some magical ability to win. [Because] Battier...seems to help the team in all sorts of subtle, hard-to-measure ways that appear to violate his personal interests."

Subtle, hard-to-measure ways.

Lewis continues:

Battier's game is a weird combination of obvious weaknesses and nearly invisible strengths. When he is on the court, his teammates get better, often a lot better, and his opponents get worse—often a lot worse. He may not grab huge numbers of rebounds, but he has an uncanny ability to improve his teammates' rebounding. He doesn't shoot much, but when he does, he takes only the most efficient shots...

On defense, although he routinely guards the NBA's most prolific scorers, he significantly reduces shooting percentages. [We] call him Lego. When he's on the court, all the pieces start to fit together.

Husbands, children, and coworkers may not understand what it is exactly that we do. Yet because of who we are and what we do, whether in our home, community, or workplace, things magically work. Like Shane Battier, our very presence seems to just make everything and everyone work better together. It's hard to put your finger on it, but in my experience this "magic" of bringing people together and enhancing their strengths is a talent that many women seem to have. It's one reason we are so good at being a safe haven and playing a supporting role, but it's a talent that we can use for great good when we dust off our dreams and put on our Batman suit.

Nurturing ourselves, or dreaming, is the respite we need, so that we can continue to nurture others. And we'll know when we aren't doing enough because each of us has a boundary. When that boundary is crossed, we become resentful. Our doing can become about manipulating others into getting what we want. Our resentment can turn to anger, which, if left unchecked, can become rage and, more often than not, depression. Depression is rage turned inward. If we find ourselves angry, it's important to listen and wonder why. Anger tells us something is amiss, that something or someone (possibly ourselves) needs to be attended to. Anger or sadness can be a warning that our boundaries have been crossed. A great example of establishing boundaries comes from April Perry, a codirector of The Power of Moms (powerofmoms.com). She considers each day of motherhood to be a privilege, but she's often overwhelmed by the workload. As one of her daughters commented, "Mom, you know how you said you wanted to be the kind of mother who makes brownies every day? Well, the only thing *we* do every day is empty the dishwasher!"

April Perry: *Mommy Is a Person*

Mothers have an amazing capacity to love and care for their families. We don't expect our lives to be unchanged once we have children. Their laughter, smiles, darling antics, and the love that radiates from them (even as infants) are worth whatever it takes. The challenge comes when we start to feel like martyrs and forget that behind the snuggling, carpools, discipline, and endless procession of meals, we are still women.

The first time I remember wondering where "April" had gone was during a lunch with three of my children. Before I had even gotten past the crust of the sandwich I had made for myself, someone wanted a refill of milk. Another needed a side of cheese, and a third wanted the sandwich opened, not folded. I didn't like the frustration I felt, so the next time we all sat down to eat, I did things a little differently.

After serving everyone their food (and a napkin and drink and utensils), I asked, "Does everyone have everything they need? I'd like you to tell me right now because I'm going to sit down and eat my food. I'm not getting up again until I'm done because Mommy is a person. Let's say that all together: '*Mommy...is...a person.*' That's right. I get to eat, too. Everyone is all set? Great!"

It took a few days of training before my children stopped asking for things mid-meal, but my declaration worked. Sometimes I have to stifle a giggle at the dinner table because I'm deliriously excited to actually eat a whole plate of food in one sitting. Now my son will say, "Mom, can I have another roll with jelly, when you're done eating?" I want to kiss him on his head and say, "Bless you, child!"

What surprised me was how quickly everyone agreed to my personhood. My children want me to be happy. They're really not trying to be overly demanding. It's just that they're children. They let me know what they need. I simply need to do the same.

CONNECTING EMOTIONALLY

April is learning to set boundaries, to nurture herself so that she can nurture others—to make things magically work. What's interesting is that the very reason those boundaries are so difficult is because of emotional attunement. While being perceived as feminine only within the context of a relationship—whether we're someone's mother, daughter, or sister—and when we are giving something to someone else can circumscribe our dreams, our connectedness can also move our dreams forward.

For example, because we are emotionally responsive to others, we generally know how to build relationships, and we sense when we need to give up something to maintain a relationship. We're rarely *asked* to give something up, we just know. In the biblical account of Abigail, one important thing happens so quickly we could miss it. Nabal and David get into their ego-driven skirmish. Abigail doesn't want her husband to die. She needs to fix the situation, and fast. She knows exactly what to do. There isn't a long passage in the Bible about how she deliberated.

These scenarios happen so often we probably don't recognize them. For example: your husband isn't sure what step his career should take or how he should navigate that next move. You know what he is capable of and how to help him do it. Or, your child is struggling in school and you intuitively know how to troubleshoot, whether academically or socially. Another scenario: you sit in a meeting at work or in the community. Others hear what's said, but you're picking up on what isn't said. Consequently, you can move things forward in a way others cannot.

In Orson Scott Card's book *The Call of Earth*, the character Hushith "lives in the constant awareness of all the connections and relationships among the people around her. Having a websense is the most important thing in her life, as she watches people connect and detach from each other, forming communities and dissolving them."

Yes is the key word of connection. Women know how to say *yes*, to connect to others and build relationships. This feminine strength of building relationships serves us well, whether within our homes or in the community.

During an especially daunting period in my career, my friend Stacey Petrey referred me to Harvard Business School professor Boris Groysberg's article "How Star Women Build Portable Skills," a study indicating that women are generally more successful than men in moving from one job to another because of the portability of our skills.

Groysberg states, "Women have learned how to build external networks of clients, associates, and other professionals outside the organizations that remain intact when they depart...Not because women set out to do this but because they [women] are often marginalized, left out of the office power structure, and have to fight institutional barriers, so they build external networks out of necessity."

This was precisely what I was unwittingly doing in order to make things work at work. I needed to get my job done, and I found that I wasn't getting the resources I needed within my firm. So I got creative and started constructing networks outside my firm. In the process, I acquired a competency that has become one of my greatest strengths.

MANAGING FORMAL POWER

None of what I've said means we don't need to gain skills. Nor does it mean that formal or explicit power doesn't matter, especially when it comes to dreaming. It does.

I'm always intrigued, even eager, to see *Forbes'* list of "The World's 100 Most Powerful Women." In compiling this list, the editors explained that "*Forbes* looked for women who run countries, such as Angela Merkel, Chancellor of Germany, large corporations, such as Indra Nooyi, CEO of PepsiCo, or influential nonprofits, such Risa Lavizzo-Mourey, Chairman of Robert Wood Johnson Foundation. Rankings are a combination of two scores: visibility—by press mentions—and the size of the organization or country these women lead."

I love that these women have formal power. They may speak softly; people listen regardless. They also carry a big stick, or have the wherewithal, typically financial heft, to put their words into action. Wielding formal power is impressive for women, given that we are taught that women are only feminine when we are giving something to someone else. I want to do this better; we each need to do this better. There are policies that won't be implemented, business concepts that won't get funded, wrongs that won't be righted, until we do. In other words, dreaming requires us to boldly do something for ourselves, which we are not conditioned to do as women. When we recognize this stumbling block, we will be better prepared to bravely seek our dreams and actually achieve them.

ACKNOWLEDGING HOW CAPABLE WE ARE

It is important that we draw on our innate relational skills. It's also important to not allow others to convince us that we're capable only because of our particularly female strengths.

As a stock analyst I was considered effective as measured by a number of different polls of institutions, including the *Institutional Investor* poll. But it was only toward the end of my decade as an analyst that I began to believe I was good. I excelled at brokering meetings between CEOs and clients (potential investors in their companies), at marketing my ideas, and at anticipating client needs—all things that women are expected to do well—and these skills were devalued within my firm. Though I was good at building the models, analyzing the companies, and picking stocks, on more than one occasion colleagues would pejoratively remark, "Whitney is successful because of her soft skills." It took me a long time to learn to ignore these snarky remarks, to recognize that clients paid Merrill Lynch for access to my research because I was a valuable resource to them. Being able to work with me was important, even critical, but "nice" on its own wouldn't have been enough.

In the book *If You've Been a Mother You Can Do Anything*, author Ann Crittenden makes a similar point. "What could be a greater transformational act than turning a drooling, demanding baby into a thinking, compassionate, hard-working, law-abiding adult? Clearly the parents who accomplish this, who help a child develop his or her fullest potential are the original transformative leaders." I would add that parents, and mothers in particular, sell ourselves short if we buy into the premise that parenting well is just about the "soft skills."

APPRECIATING PATIENCE AND PERSPECTIVE

Another feminine strength is patience. Most women have the experience of sacrificing resources and time to help their fathers or husbands be what they are going to be. There's a historical reason for this. Men were traditionally the breadwinners and, therefore, a family's resources were allocated to making sure he could win the bread.

The experience of most women is very different. Our attention is divided. Often because of our feminine strength of doing for others, the dreams we cherish, beyond attending to those we love, are pursued part-time or delayed. And certainly our dream of seeing our children grow into happy, responsible adults takes decades to play out. Patience is therefore required. There are pieces being put into place, but we can't quite see how everything fits. As with a puzzle, the pieces eventually come together beautifully. Remember—Julia Child was in her thirties when she started culinary school. She was in her forties when she became a cooking instructor and in her fifties when *Mastering the Art of French Cooking* was published. Sometimes our dreams take a while to unfold.

Saren Loosli received a BA from Wellesley College and MEd from Harvard, and is one of the founders of The Power of Moms (powerofmoms.com). Through the gifts of patience and perspective, Saren has been able to direct her passion for solving big problems in the third world toward improving her local community and helping other moms find joy in motherhood.

Saren Loosli: *The Power of Moms*

I studied third world development in my undergraduate years, then studied what education is and what more it could be for my master's degree. During my years of academia I thought I had figured out a whole lot of brilliant solutions to many vital issues.

But somehow I never quite got in the position to implement my ideas. I did some cool things: I worked in orphanages in Eastern Europe, was involved with humanitarian aid in Kenya and Bolivia, ran volunteer-promotion efforts nationwide, set up programs in needy schools...then I started having children.

Because my fertility clock was ticking when I finally found "Mr. Right," we started our family quickly, and the kids came in rapid succession. Thanks to a surprise set of twins, I had five children in just five years.

While I loved all my children dearly, and was so grateful that my dream of having a family came true, mothering so many small children was overwhelming. As I struggled to meet the basic needs of my children, I saw my vision of changing the larger world drift further and further away. I crammed bits and pieces of work for various worthy causes in between naps and diaper changes and story times (part-time training and consulting, service work for my church, helping a nonprofit serving Bulgarian orphanages get off the ground). But mostly, my life consisted of doing rather mundane and often unpleasant things for lots of noisy, messy, wonderful people with many mutually exclusive needs. Wasn't I meant to do something more?

One day I read a quote by Mother Teresa that stuck with me: "We can do no great things, only small things with great love." Motherhood is perhaps the greatest example of a long, long string of small things that, done with great love and extra thought, can have ripple effects that go on for generations. I came to realize that maybe my "cause," my purpose in life, was right under my nose. Perhaps mothering my own kids, helping make the schools in my own community better, being a good neighbor and friend, and learning from and helping the other mothers around me was a much "grander" cause than any other I could pursue.

My children are informed about world issues and they pray at night for the orphans in Bulgaria that we do a fundraiser for each Christmas. But I hope they're also learning something it took me a whole lot of years to figure out: I now know that doing little things to better the world immediately around you, and helping with the things you're already *part of,* is vital and beautiful, and often more satisfying than trying to impact big groups and sweeping causes.

Taking treats to a lonely neighbor is just as important as

sending money to a lonely orphan. Offering friendship to a left-out kid at school is just as important as giving food to a hungry child in Africa. Volunteering in my children's classrooms and helping them with their homework is just as important as changing education systems, and helping bright, motivated mothers find one another and share what they know is just as important as helping nonprofits to pool their resources and knowledge.

The micro matters, *a lot*. The macro doesn't happen without the micro. The little things really do count. You and I can change the world by changing our world, one person, one mother, one family at a time, starting right here with you and me.

Saren had dreams that seemed in conflict—being a full-time mother and trying to bring about significant change in the poorest countries in the world. Like many women, she has a strong desire to improve the world, but rather than put that dream on hold while caring for the needs of her young family, she is finding a way to pursue her dream in a different way, on a different scale. I have no doubt that some day Saren will come back to her original dream of tackling big problems in the third world, but she has the perspective to understand and enjoy the dreams she is accomplishing today.

CHERISHING FEMININE STRENGTHS

In Rick Riordan's book *The Sea of Monsters*, the second in a series of children's novels loosely based on ancient Greek mythology, the magical tree that guards Camp Half-Blood has been poisoned. Percy Jackson, a half-blood son of Poseidon, and Annabeth, the half-blood daughter of Athena, have only days to find the Golden

Fleece, the one magical item that will heal the tree before Camp Half-Blood is overrun by monsters.

After the Golden Ram was sacrificed, the Golden Fleece hung on a tree in the middle of the kingdom. Riordan's Annabeth explains, "The Fleece brought prosperity to the land; animals stopped getting sick. Plants grew better. Farmers had bumper crops. Plagues never visited. That's why Jason wanted the Fleece. It can revitalize any land where it's placed. It cures sickness, strengthens nature, cleans up pollution."

In the Psyche myth, which is similar to Riordan's story, Psyche's second task requires that she gather fleece that has the power to heal. To obtain the fleece she must wait until sundown when the rams disperse. She can then safely pick strands of fleece off the brambles. Psyche's ability to acquire the fleece without being crushed is a metaphor for every woman's task of gaining power without losing her innate sense of connectedness and compassion. The fleece symbolizes the power to get things done in a way that gives life to and revitalizes others.

As we look to identify our strengths it's important to examine our identities, including our gender. As women, we are sometimes denied opportunities, as was the case with Eunice Shriver, founder of the Special Olympics. Her father was reported to have said she would have made a fine politician, had she been a man; but we also gain opportunities as we tap into our fearlessness on behalf of those we love, as we explore our emotional attunement, our innate relational skills, and our long-term perspective. Our feminine strengths may not always be acknowledged or even recognized. As Seth Godin writes, "The easier to quantify, the less it is worth." When we come to understand our particular abilities and talents as women, we have another tool to help us discover and achieve our dreams.

VALUING OUR FEMININITY...

People used to look out on the playground and say that the boys were playing soccer and the girls were doing nothing...But the girls weren't doing nothing—they were talking. They were talking about the world to one another. And they became very expert about that in a way the boys did not.

—Carol Gilligan, American psychologist

- Have you ever considered that your tenacity on behalf of loved ones is a feminine strength?
- How do these emotional attunement and relational skills define your dreams?
- Is it possible that you, like Julia Blake, are already living your dream?
- Are your dreams giving life to both you and those you love?

10

RIGHTSIZE YOUR DREAMS

The story of Psyche (see chapter 3) focuses on feminine development, and on the characteristics women must acquire to become complete. Psyche could only be reunited with her beloved after completing four tasks. The difficulty of the assignments could have paralyzed her, and each task required more than she felt capable of. Likewise, it is only through navigating our own challenges that we grow into the women we envision ourselves to be.

Like Psyche, modern women must establish priorities and sift through possible dreams in the face of conflicting feelings and competing loyalties. Learning to trust our judgment is one of the first skills we must learn, to truly grow up. Determining priorities may require that we "sleep on it," letting our subconscious mind, a repository of our deeply held principles and beliefs—work things out. As we learn to trust our intuition, providential guidance comes and clarity on how to properly size our dreams emerges. Consider the story of Rebecca Nielsen, a mother of twin girls, who holds an MBA from Harvard Business School, and was previously a senior director with UnitedHealth Group.

Rebecca Edwards Nielsen: *Rightsizing My Dream*

Years ago I set a goal to run the Red Cross. I then determined that attending business school and gaining management skills in the private sector were important steps to qualifying myself to lead a major nongovernmental organization (NGO). When I called my college chemistry professor for a letter of recommendation, he replied, "Rebecca, I don't envision you in business. I see you running the Red Cross."

I had to smile. I shared that dream on my business school application and in my entrance interview. After each class I wrote in my journal about how my education in brand management, strategy, controls, or finance would serve me in the not-for-profit arena—and I kept the dream tangible: someday I would run the Red Cross. After business school I spent five years working in the health care industry developing general management skills.

Fast forward: I am now a full-time mother of beautiful twin girls. Swept up in this dream—which is more purposeful and joyful than I expected—I think more about catching up on sleep than fundraising for disaster relief. However, I heed Langston Hughes' caution that dreams deferred can dry up like a raisin in the sun, and welcome the chance to reflect on this goal. I've planted some stakes in the ground as I start this process of reassessing: I savor this time with my girls and I want to spend the bulk of my time with my children for years to come.

Although I now have competing dreams that need to make room for each other, I am still enthusiastic about making strides in both—but not necessarily at the same time. Within days of beginning to write this blog post, I learned of the passing of my aunt. She enjoyed a rich family life and accomplished remarkable professional goals. She did it in stages. When her youngest child started kindergarten, she started writing. In the years that followed, she published twelve books. Some of her most notable works came from experiences with her children.

I anticipate that there will be a season in my life when I will chase my dream of running the Red Cross, and that my experiences as a mother will provide valuable fodder and perspective in championing humanitarian relief.

My dream may need to be rightsized, as I won't have a traditional management résumé, but I am not disheartened. If I am not in a position to lead an established NGO, I will be able to serve on nonprofit boards, volunteer in humanitarian relief on a local level, and follow my parents' example of devoting time to an extended humanitarian mission abroad. I may need to become a nonprofit entrepreneur, and bootstrap my own effort to make a difference. Although my goal may change, its essence—to use my skills to champion humanitarian relief—is still within reach.

MOURNING DEFERRED OR DERAILED DREAMS

Rebecca is currently in the process of rightsizing her dreams, but it's not always possible. My friend Sally Harker commented to me one day over lunch, "I love nearly everything about your blog, especially reading stories of women who are achieving their dreams, but what about the women whose dreams go unfulfilled?" To humorously underscore her point, she sent me a link to a *New Yorker* cartoon in which a well-dressed woman asks a clerk at an upscale department store, "What would you suggest to fill the dark, empty spaces in my soul?"

I'll answer with a rhetorical question—have you achieved all of your dreams? I haven't. Do you have empty spaces? Empty spaces that never get filled—at least on a timetable you like? I do. When dreams go unfulfilled, there is sadness; we need to honor that sadness. Isn't it also true that in the effort to fill our empty spaces, we begin to write our stories, characterize ourselves as heroes, and make our greatest contributions? Consider, for instance, Jill Hubbard Bowman, an intellectual property (IP) attorney in Austin, Texas, who publishes a legal blog, *IP Law for Startups,* iplawforstartups.com, and an inspiring career website for young women, lookilulu.com.

Jill Hubbard Bowman: *Unexpected Twists and Turns*

I had a dream to be a trial attorney who would fight big legal battles and win. And then my dream was derailed by a twin pregnancy that almost killed me. Literally. It was a shock and awe pregnancy. It caused the death, destruction, and rebirth of my identity and legal career.

I was working as an intellectual property litigation attorney for a large law firm in Chicago when a pregnancy with twins caused my heart to fail. After fifteen years of infertility, the twin pregnancy was an unexpected surprise. Heart failure because of the pregnancy was an even bigger shock. The toll on my legal career was even more unexpected.

Although I was fortunate to survive without a heart transplant, I eventually realized that I needed a career transplant. As my heart function recovered, I valiantly tried to cling to my career dream and do the hard work I loved. But the long hours and travel necessary for trial work were too much for my physical self. I was exhausted with chronic chest pain, two clinging toddlers, and a disgruntled husband. I was tired of being tired. My law firm was exceptionally supportive but I didn't have the stamina to keep all of the pieces of my life together.

Overwhelmed, I let go of my original dream. I backed down,

retrenched, and regrouped. I took a year off from legal work to rest, recover, spend time with my toddlers, and open myself to new possibilities.

During my hiatus, I rethought my legal career. I had long discussions with other women who were juggling motherhood and career dreams. I identified the things that gave me energy and passion, including counseling, sharing information, and writing. I realized that I was motivated to help people, especially women, avoid suffering, whether from ignorance of the law or simply because they aren't aware of the opportunities available to them.

In my repose, I also took stock of my assets. I'm a walking treatise on intellectual property law. I've done intellectual property cleanup and dispute resolution for many years and I've seen the variety of mistakes that companies make. Moreover, in more than twenty-five years, I've learned a lot about professional careers and finding work that is fulfilling and rewarding based on individual strengths and interests.

Revitalized and healthy, I started dreaming new dreams. I saw ways that I could make a significant contribution by sharing what I've learned. I decided to refocus my legal practice on counseling and helping start-up companies avoid liability and protect their intellectual property.

To share some of what I know, I started a blog, *IP Law for Startups*, where I teach basic lessons on trade secrets, trademarks, copyrights, and patents and give tips for avoiding the biggest blunders that destroy the value of intellectual assets. Few start-up companies, especially women-owned companies that rarely get venture capital funding, can afford the expensive hourly rates of a large law firm to the get the critical information they need. I feel deeply rewarded when I help a company create a strategy that protects the value of their company and supports their business dreams.

Further, I had a dream to help young women see their career possibilities. In partnership with my sister, Julie Simmons, I created lookilulu.com, a website where women share their insights, career paths, and ways they have integrated motherhood with their professional pursuits. When my sister and I were growing up on a farm, we had a hard time seeing that women could have rewarding careers. With Lookilulu® we want to help young women see what we couldn't see: that dreams are not linear—they take many twists and unexpected turns.

As I've learned the hard way, dreams change and shift as life happens. I've learned the value of continuing to dream new dreams after other dreams are derailed. I'm sure I'll have many more dreams in my future. I've learned to be open to new and unexpected opportunities.

By way of postscript, Jill writes, "I didn't grow up planning to be lawyer. As a girl growing up in a small rural town, I was afraid to dream. I loved science, but rather than pursuing medical school, I opted for low-paying laboratory jobs, planning to quit when I had children. But then I couldn't have children. As I awakened to the possibility that dreaming was an inalienable right, even for me, I started law school when I was thirty; intellectual property combines my love of law and science."

As a young girl, Jill's rightsizing involved mustering the courage to expand her dreams, to dream outside of her box. Once she had children, she again transformed her dreams. In many ways her dreams are bigger and aim to help more people than before the twists and turns in her life's path.

Lori Lyn Price, a biostatician at Tufts Medical Center and a professional genealogist (bridgingthepast.com), has a dream that hasn't quite happened yet: to marry and become a mother.

Lori Lyn Price: *Bridging from the Past to Her Future*

I entered college with the expectation that I would marry while there, and with a firm determination to graduate in spite of that. I was consequently taken completely by surprise when I woke up one spring morning with no marital prospects and graduation only a few weeks away.

Although obtaining my degree was important to me, I had planned my career as a stay-at-home mom, never entertaining other plans or a job outside the home. However, with graduation looming I needed to make a decision. Unsure whether I wanted to enter graduate school or find a job, I took an internship at the Cleveland Clinic Foundation to give myself time to think about this unexpected turn of events.

Twelve years after taking that internship, I remain single, and yet I look back at all the opportunities that have come my way. Working at the Cleveland Clinic, a prestigious medical research center, opened the way for me to work in practically any other medical research institution. My boss at the Cleveland Clinic offered me opportunities that were unusual for someone with my experience. I eventually earned a master's degree in statistics and moved to Boston to work at Tufts Medical Center.

I've also had the flexibility to travel extensively, in the United States and abroad, to Egypt, Israel, Portugal, Mexico, and Canada. I've pursued additional degrees and explored diverse hobbies that include photography, card-making, jewelry-making, and genealogy. If I had married in college, there may not have been time or money for these pursuits.

More recently, I decided to return to graduate school to study history. As an undergraduate, I considered double-majoring in history and statistics, but eventually opted for just statistics, which turned out to be a wise choice: my career as a biostatistician is challenging, pays reasonably well, and, most importantly, I enjoy it.

I'm also combining my knowledge of history and genealogy to start a lecturing business for genealogists, Bridging the Past, which provides context on how historical events affected daily life in colonial New England. One of my favorite lectures is a discussion of extraordinary colonial women, which contrasts their life experiences with those of modern-day women.

My life is very different than I envisioned it as a teenager. I thought I would be a wife and mother. It has been difficult to see all five of my younger sisters marry and have children while I remain single. And yet, as I've pursued the opportunities before me, I am discovering new dreams and a life that is full and happy in unexpected ways.

Lori Lyn is finding new and different ways to achieve her dreams. She acknowledges the pain of an important dream (of marrying and having children) being unfulfilled, yet recognizes how many other dreams have been made possible because she is single. Often, circumstances beyond our control force us to rightsize our dreams, as well as to simply realize that we aren't always in control.

I came to this realization after having a miscarriage. When my son was two, we were ready for another baby and I got pregnant without any trouble, just as I had the first time. My carefully laid plans were swept away when I miscarried just one month into my pregnancy. Emily Nielson, who holds a BA in music from the University of Massachusetts–Boston, shares the insights she learned about derailed dreams after experiencing a miscarriage of her own.

Emily Nielson: *The Beauty of Seasons*

On an average fall day, you can find me in my garden, tasting, smelling, and enjoying. It's not just me that loves the garden; at any given time, a child will have a handful of green beans and seedy tomato juice dripping everywhere. Or my husband might be there. Our garden is kind of an extension of our home, lots of good food and love.

In years past, either my husband or I have taken charge of the garden, depending on who had more time and energy that year to be the garden's "keeper." That person plans the garden, then plants and tends it, with the help of the children. Seems simple enough, right? Well, I discovered it's not that simple, and this year my garden is very different, for a reason you probably wouldn't expect. In February, I suffered a miscarriage at sixteen weeks gestation.

I had spent sixteen weeks producing the most precious, beautiful fruit that can be produced by humankind. I had planned and nurtured and was tending to the precious fruit. Then, when I believed I had no reason not to enjoy my eventual harvest, my precious fruit died. Just like that. No harvest, no fruit. No sweet, soft, new baby that would be mine.

A few months later, when my husband and I began to discuss planting the garden, I was apathetic, tired, and weary. Gardens are a lot of work. But now that some time has passed, I realize that I didn't want to put my heart and soul into nurturing something that would take a long time to grow and then might die. I didn't want to be the "keeper" of the garden. Meanwhile, my husband was busy and dealing with his own sadness, so he didn't plant the garden either.

All summer and fall, I have missed the garden. This week,

when I went into the backyard to grab something for the kids, my eyes wandered over to the faded, empty patch surrounded by ivy and multicolored roses, and felt the familiar pang of wishing we had taken the time to properly plant and care for the garden.

In that moment, quietly but clearly, a thought came to my mind. It was a hopeful, beautiful thought that I credit to God— a thought that reminded me of the beauty of seasons. Seasons start and end, come and go. My dirt patch of a garden, now that it was November, wasn't barren because we had neglected it. All gardens were barren at that moment because the season was over.

And next spring would be a completely new season, untouched by the misfortune of any past seasons: new blossoms on the trees, seedlings sprouting. Joy and relief overcame me. We could start over with our garden and in a few months it could be resiliently returned to its former glory. Almost simultaneously, I realized that, like our garden, our family could recover from our miscarriage.

As I now carry another unborn child, I am grateful to have learned that while some seasons bring sadness, many will bring happiness. The bitterness of one season can lead to sweeter anticipation and sweeter enjoyment of seasons to come.

Emily dared to dream of a new baby, a wonderful addition for her family to love and cherish, and very sadly, her dream died. As we dare to dream, we are preparing to birth a new piece of ourselves. Something wonderful is going to be. But sometimes the dream dies. And this can be terribly sad.

We eventually make meaning of the experience and tell our story. After we grieve, we pick ourselves up and dream again. Which is precisely what Shawni Pothier, a mother and a blogger

(71toes.com), has done. Shawni recently launched the I Love Lucy Project to help raise funds for research to fight blindness. Shawni's youngest daughter has been diagnosed with a syndrome that causes vision loss.

Shawni Pothier: *I Love Lucy Project*

At the birth of each of my five babies I was completely euphoric. I sat in my hospital bed with them and gazed deeply into their eyes as my heart swelled up to the size of a watermelon with pure love. Those babies were my dream come true...the dream to be a mother.

As I sat there soaking them in, I dreamed of a life for each of them as full and rewarding as could be. Of course, as mothers we never dream of our children to having to deal with health issues or trials. I dream of only the good: confidence, friends, marriage, and family.

But my big dreams shifted dramatically with the birth of my fifth baby, Lucy. She politely introduced me to *real life*.

Not only was she born with an extra toe and a couple of birthmarks, she was delayed. Even at three months old she hadn't smiled, despite my most impressive attempts to strain my own smile muscles at her. She couldn't roll over for what seemed like forever. She couldn't sit up for very long, and at almost two years old, she still wasn't walking.

My husband and I worried our hearts out. As we struggled through doctor after doctor, trying to figure it out, I realized I had been living in a dream world with my first four kids. Every one of them was right on, developmentally. One week they learned to play peek-a-boo. The next they learned to give kisses. Then they started saying words, which were added to one by one, then ten by ten. This was normal.

Lucy qualified for speech therapy, then physical therapy. She had MRIs and hearing tests that required sedation since she was so feisty. I became best friends with the nurses at the blood lab who helped me hold poor Lucy down endless times to draw blood for various tests ordered by the geneticist.

One winter day last year, we got a call we knew was coming. Lucy was diagnosed with Bardet-Biedl, a rare syndrome that causes heart and kidney issues, obesity, and, most heart-wrenching to us, blindness.

Everything was claustrophobic; my thoughts swirled. I worried about my husband, who wants to always "fix" things that go wrong, and here was something he couldn't "fix." I worried about our other kids getting the attention they needed, given Lucy's needs. I worried about all her health issues, the myriad things that could go wrong.

My heart sank when people started talking to us about the Foundation for the Blind and Braille, classes for young kids to learn to walk with canes, heart and kidney problems associated with this syndrome, the possibility of diabetes, and kidney transplants.

This syndrome was not part of the "dream" I envisioned for my daughter as I lay in my hospital bed when she was born. What about all the things I dreamed she'd do? I went from dreaming big to letting fear seep in. Would Lucy be able to function in life? Would she have friends? Would she depend on us forever? And what about my dream that she'd someday be a wife and mother?

During the year since Lucy's diagnosis, I have been smacked in the face with the realization that it is through our struggles that we grow the most. And that we all have struggles. We all have dreams that haven't become a reality. Gradually, our challenges shape us, and dreams we hadn't anticipated emerge.

Lucy is a sweet, strong-willed, chubby three-year-old who

captures the hearts of all who meet her. Her life is not going in the direction I had hoped for when I cradled her as a newborn, but she is influencing many, giving hope along the way. I'm learning to be flexible, to recognize that when a dream reaches a dead end, an alternate dream can and will emerge.

As my dream for Lucy shifts, my dream as a mother has shifted as well. All the wonderful things I hoped for are still there, but fighting for Lucy and against blindness, especially Lucy's type of blindness, which there may be a cure for, has lit a fire within me.

It is a joy to have something bigger than myself and my family to fight for.

Shawni's experience is not uncommon among parents—we all have dreams for our children, and whether through the circumstance of a genetic anomaly or simply our child's individual agency, sometimes those dreams die, or at least shift. In this circumstance, Shawni found peace and energy in redirecting her dreams. Are there dreams in your life that need to shift?

REDIRECTING DREAMS

Several years ago, I had a black-tie event to attend. For the first time ever I had a dress made. It was a luxury, I'll admit, but it was a liberating experience. I chose fabric that matched my skin tone, hair, and personality. I selected a pattern that would look good on my body. Most lovely of all was the moment when the seamstress sized the skirt of the dress to me: my waist, my body, my measurements. It wasn't about my fitting into the dress, but about the dress fitting me. The same experience can be had with our dreams. They can be off-the-rack, but with some effort on our part, our dreams can be tailored to us: from our talents, competencies, principles, and identities—our strengths—we can create the right dream for us.

More often than not, rightsizing a dream involves reducing the scope of one dream to make room for another, but it's important that we are also open to supersizing a dream. Take, for example, Megan Nelson who was wavering on applying for law school, but after we spoke, she's not only going to apply to safety schools, she's applying to schools that feel slightly beyond her grasp.

Or consider, Melissa D'Arabian, the winner of season five of *The Next Food Network Star*, who beat out thousands of hopefuls. Prior to entering the competition, Melissa was a stay-at-home mom to her four young daughters. She dared to dream as she entered the competition, but she doubted herself. She was a good cook, and had worked as a live-in cook to put herself through business school, but she was not professionally trained. Many, including Melissa herself, dismissed her as just a stay-at-home mom, a home cook. Over the course of a few months, we saw her transform from a woman full of self-doubt to one who, in daring, supersized her dream and realized just how capable she is.

Though this book is about giving ourselves permission to dream, to think bigger, and, in effect, supersize our dreams, often we find ourselves needing to rightsize, as dreams die or are deferred. Or we need to downsize, reducing the scope of one dream to make room for another. Adjusting our dreams, sifting through possibilities, and establishing priorities in the face of conflicting feelings and competing loyalties is a monumental task, one that will require that we draw on our intuition, our deepest sense of self, core beliefs, and principles. But if we'll take on that task, we can stitch together a dream that is a perfect fit.

OFF-THE-RACK OR TAILOR-MADE...

Be careful who you let define your good.
> —Lois McMaster Bujold, science fiction writer

- Why is learning to sift through possibilities and to prioritize them one of our key developmental tasks as women?
- Do you have any dreams that are currently intersecting? How are you prioritizing them?
- If you are deferring a dream, have you considered keeping a journal that outlines how what you are doing now will help you achieve your dream?
- Some dreams that we all deserve may go unrealized indefinitely. Do we honor that loss?
- Unrealized dreams may also lead to unimagined opportunities, new dreams, and happiness. What unrealized dreams have freed up the resources (time, money, energy) that you can reinvest in your current dreams?
- Is it time to redirect or shift one of your dreams?
- Is there something that you used to love to do that you've set aside? Is it possible that you can combine your childhood skills with the ones you've since acquired, to tell yourself a new story—one that is fresh and relevant to you today?
- Do you have a dream that needs to be supersized? What do you need to make this happen? And if you are holding back—why?

PART THREE

DO

Making Your Dreams Happen

Whatever you can do or dream you can, begin it.
Boldness has genius, power and magic in it.
—*Goethe, eighteenth century German author*

Make things happen—that's what women do. You are unstoppable when you are doing for others, helping them achieve their dreams. But what about your newly discovered or re-discovered dreams? You've embraced the necessity of dreaming, you even know what your dream is, but you're daunted by the start. First off, throw out your conventional planning, because dreaming is discovery-driven. Where you end up won't be where you began, but you'll never get there if you don't begin. Next, assemble a dare to dream team—a group of mentors and experts, cheerleaders and fellow dreamers who understand what you're trying to do and will help get your dream off the ground. Consider the women in the pages of this book as a part of that team. Then embrace your constraints. You are likely already quite adept at making do with what you have. Just as your dreams may be right in front of you, many of the resources you need are often on hand as well. Go ahead and date dreams, lots of them—you don't need to commit to every dream you date. And finally, be bold, be daring. As you fully become the hero of your story, possibilities will unfold, you'll glimpse your own magnificence, and remarkable things will begin to happen.

11

EMBRACE DISCOVERY

In part 2, we began to give our dreams definition, to animate their barely visible contours. This process began with some prep work, of learning to claim a central place in our lives and making space for our dreams. We then identified our strengths—which spring from innate talents, acquired competencies, bedrock beliefs, and our identities as women—and examined how these strengths inform, and even direct, our dreams. We also talked about the importance of rightsizing our dreams by trusting our judgment.

DISCOVERY-DRIVEN DREAMING

Dreaming is a discovery-driven process. We envision something that's not yet fully formed, and as we set short-term goals around that dream, our dream takes shape. We almost always think we know where we're going, but in reality we don't. Fortunately, we're in good company.

According to Columbia University professor Amar V. Bhide, for 90 percent of all successful new businesses, the strategy the founders initially pursued didn't lead to the business's success. Rephrased for our purposes: in 90 percent of all successful dreams, our first plan of action will not achieve our dream. To take that point even further, consider that the dream we *think* will make us happy rarely does. Consider, for example, Jean Knight Pace, who holds an M.F.A. in creative writing and is a mother of four living in Indiana. She has discovered, to her surprise, that one of her deepest dreams is to become a *maker of a home*, including becoming a great cook (tastycheapskate .blogspot.com).

Jean Knight Pace: *The Tasty Cheapskate*

As a girl born a generation after the feminist revolution, it seemed I could dream any dream I wished. I could become a doctor, lawyer, singer, or writer. I could travel. I could teach. The world was wide open. Except in one small, candle-less corner: I could not develop domestic skills. They were out of vogue. To learn to cook or sew, to think or talk about having and caring for children, it just wasn't something my girlfriends and I did. And it certainly wasn't something our teachers or school counselors encouraged us to do. So even though I had a weird obsession with cooking shows, even though when I traveled it was the one thing I was willing to spend a little money on, I never learned to cook (or even really eat, always worrying about my figure).

Then, after two degrees, travel, work, and service in my church, I got married. And, sure enough, along came a baby in a baby carriage. And I really liked him. I loved him—unabashedly and desperately. Which surprised me just a touch. What surprised me even more were all the dreams that opened up for me when I quit my job to stay home with my wee and sleepy infant.

Strangely, I felt I had more time than I had ever had in my life before—a life that had been filled with school and work and an unhealthy obsession with perfection and overachievement.

I didn't start out trying to cook brains like Julia Child had. I kept it simple. I began with Hamburger Helper. I stood over the meat as it changed in color and aroma, and it struck something in me—something primal, homey, and lush. I had cooked it. I would feed us. It was quite similar to the feeling I had had when I first breast-fed my son. It was a young version of the feeling I would have when eventually I gardened and grew the things we would eat. And it was, frankly, crazy-intoxicating.

From that first simple meal, I moved on gradually (very gradually) to more complicated things. I made eggs, to which I added tomatoes, garlic powder, and onion powder, and which I served with a bit of salsa. I then made some mashed potatoes from scratch one day. And, oh, they were so much better than the instant ones.

And suddenly my dream was something that, in all my studying and working and worrying and degree-getting, I had never thought to dream. It applied to kids. It applied to our home, or our mini-homestead, as I liked to think of it. And it applied to cooking, to food. In time and with experience, my cooking became more experimental and more creative. My life, though seemingly narrower and more restrictive, felt fuller than it ever had.

I started e-mailing recipes to friends and family. I started finding advice and more recipes online. I couldn't stop reading about food, gardening, animals, and the land. And with each pregnancy I learned to listen more to what my body had to say about food; I continually traded recipes back and forth with friends and family.

And then one night there was the perfect storm of ideas. I'd been trying to knock about $200 off our food budget—no simple task when you love to cook. I'd been thinking about comments politicians and journalists had made about how the poor could not possibly afford or have the time to prepare "good food." At the same time, my husband, who is a paramedic, and I had been discussing the ill effects of smoking on people and society. I wondered if people could eat on the amount of money they spent on cigarettes. And then I wondered if my family of six could. It was an exciting, terrifying, mind-whirring sort of prospect. And I liked it.

Within six months, *The Tasty Cheapskate* was born. It contained recipes, commentary on food and home life, and a budgetary challenge: our family of six would try to eat on $6 a day. It's an obsession, I admit, but one I try to keep in check. Because one thing I've learned in finding and living my most verdant dreams is that they might go unrealized if a person doesn't have a little time to sit on the sidelines, preferably with some good food in hand and a chubby toddler on her lap.

Jean Knight Pace's current dreams are not the ones she started with, but as she has dared to become the hero of her story, to nose her way toward what she finds herself happiest doing, Jean is living her "most verdant dreams."

Professor Rita Gunther McGrath of Columbia University describes discovery-driven planning as follows: "When one is operating in arenas with significant amounts of uncertainty, a different approach than is normally used in conventional planning applies. In conventional planning, the correctness of a plan is generally judged by how close projections come to outcomes."

Conventional planning is, in essence, about the checklist. On a school day, we may plan to wake up at 5:30 A.M., get our children ready for school, send them to school, organize a closet, do the laundry, exercise, spend a couple of hours on a project, pick up the children from school and shuttle them to after-school activities, prepare and eat dinner, do homework, read a book, go to bed. At the end of the day, we measure the correctness of our plan by how well we executed against this plan. With conventional planning, because we are pretty clear about what needs to be done and what will happen, we can allocate resources to the entire project or day in advance.

In contrast, discovery-driven planning isn't, nor can it be, about the checklist. It's assumed that the plan will change, because as new information comes to light, our plan will need to change to accommodate that information. Just think about life after having a baby. A new mother could write the book on discovery-driven planning. How can you plan with a newborn? You want to plan, and sometimes we amuse ourselves by thinking we can, but we just can't predict how any given day or night will go. You might tell yourself, "If I get enough sleep tonight, I'll be able to exercise tomorrow." But you won't know what your plan should be until you have more information (that is, how tired you are). When you have that information you can make a decision about how to allocate your resources, namely, your time. I use the example of having a newborn, but the reality is that being a parent is almost completely discovery-driven.

As we consider our lives, most of the really big questions that need to be answered involve the discovery-driven process. Take college, for instance. According to Dr. Fritz Grupe, founder of MyMajors (mymajors.com,) "80 percent of college-bound students have yet to choose a major, while 50 percent of those who do declare a major, change their majors—with many doing so two or three times during their college years." There's the 90 percent again.

My career has been discovery-driven. I was a music major who arrived in New York with no idea of what I wanted to be when I grew up, other than *not* a musician, and eventually a mother. Writing this book has been discovery-driven. I knew in sweeping terms what I wanted to say, but codifying how we discover and pursue our dreams came as I wrote. Most of us are quite capable of conventional planning. We're less schooled in, and therefore less comfortable with, discovery-driven thinking, the kind of thinking that helps us successfully pursue our dreams. That's not altogether surprising. Convention is control. Discovery is letting go.

A friend who is a psychology professor at a prestigious university in Boston recently related an experience she'd had while teaching a class of female graduating seniors. These young women had worked very hard to get into the university, and had spent more than $100,000 on their educations, but on the eve of graduation, the students were terrified. Several dissolved into tears as they pondered, *"Now what?"* My friend's observation was that these students had learned to excel at meeting concrete, measurable, short-term, *this is what I do* goals. They weren't quite as sure about how to ask and answer big, undefined questions, such as, *"What am I meant to do?"*

Graduating seniors aren't alone in their uncertainty. Most of us occasionally succumb to the terror of wondering what we're meant to do. On good days, however, we are reminded that discovery as a process to relish, and that we can trust that our intuition, and a higher power, will help us sift and sort our way to defining our life's course.

Eva Koleva Timothy, born and reared in Bulgaria, is not only leading a discovery-driven life, through her work as a photographer, but also has chronicled the journey of discovery. Her monograph *Lost in Learning* (lostinlearning.com) was published in 2010.

Eva Koleva Timothy: *Lost in Learning*

When I was a young girl, my father's stories whisked me off to lands of far away and long ago. Some of the stories were fantastic—fairy tales, stories of Arabian nights, Bulgarian folklore, and the like. Others based in European history were about Alexander the Great, Leonardo da Vinci, Christopher Columbus, and other larger-than-life figures. Although the stories were from long ago, they didn't seem so far away. Bulgaria has been at the crossroads of every major civilization for more than two millennia—and under a foreign yoke for most of that time, beginning with Alexander the Great, and then the Greeks, who were followed by the Ottoman Empire and finally the Soviet occupation.

Growing up under Communist rule, I yearned for freedom. When I told people of my dream to live in the United States, most laughed. At that time, the idea of leaving a country so tightly controlled by the Soviet bloc was ludicrous. The stories my parents told me about history's great explorers and independent thinkers helped me remain hopeful that, someday, I would come to America.

After the Berlin Wall fell, there really was a chance I could come and live in America. There was one minor obstacle: I didn't speak English and I needed to pass an English test. I was fourteen years old and had never wanted to learn anything so much in my life. I took index cards to the movie theater so that, when watching subtitled American films, I could write down the phrases I picked up from the actors. When I was caught reading Shakespeare during my Russian class, I got sent to the headmaster's office. I spoke with every American I could find, and while books had never been a favorite birthday gift, I fell in love with the huge English–Bulgarian dictionary my parents had given me for my fifteenth birthday.

I passed the exam, and, thanks to the generosity of Richard and Linda Eyre, well-regarded authorities on parenting, and the friendship of their daughter Saren, I was given the opportunity to realize my dream and study in the United States.

Twenty years later, I've embarked on another voyage of discovery, one that involves my photography. In many ways, my work today is a continuation of what I began as a teenager.

Several years ago I read *The Discoverers* by Daniel Boorstin, an historian and former head of the Library of Congress. As I read about Columbus's preparation for his journey across the ocean, and how he wrote copious notes in the margins of one of his geography books, I thought, "Wouldn't it be cool to see the book with his actual handwriting!"

At the time, I had been photographing a series of old books I had from the year our family lived in Oxford. Thinking about Columbus's geography books, I had the idea to photograph manuscripts, instruments, and artifacts in a way that would tell the story of the amazing men and women I was reading about.

And so I began. I found a copy of the *Imago Mundi,* a fourteenth-century map of the world, with Columbus' notes. I put that document together with an old compass, and the project was born. From there I visited the Harvard Collection of Scientific Instruments to photograph Renaissance-era artifacts. I acquired copies of manuscripts by Galileo, da Vinci, Sir Isaac Newton, Robert Hooke, Georg Friedrich Handel, and others. I visited antique shops to find period spectacles, prisms, a miniature spyglass, and a beautiful magnifying glass.

These lenses, which granted sight, focused light, and enabled learning during those long-ago eras, became a symbol of the project. The items also reminded me that the discoveries we now celebrate and teach were made possible because those who came before us opened their eyes to see the world with curiosity, imagination, and a desire to explore.

The wonder of a voyage of discovery is that you don't know where it will lead. How could Eva have known as a young girl that one day she really would live in the United States, have three children, and eventually photograph artifacts of the greatest discoverers of all time and compile them into an award-winning book?

Certainly, as I consider my career since I left Wall Street in 2005, it has been a journey toward something entirely different than what I had originally envisioned. In leaving, I had some idea of what I wanted to do, such as produce a television show. I pursued several ideas, none of which worked. I also became involved in two start-ups. One business failed almost immediately, the other achieved some success before ultimately failing. I wrote a business proposal for a mixed-use real estate development, which included hiring an architect to provide renderings. That project didn't go anywhere. I also dabbled at writing children's books. One of them is fully illustrated and ready to print, for another I have just the text. Concurrently, I had conversations with several of Wall Street's largest firms about returning. I thought I was serious about returning to sell-side equity research. But, in retrospect, given that I hadn't retained digital copies of my spreadsheets, my departure wasn't just a lark.

Those two years of discovery were important. I spent more time with my children, really getting to know them as I worked more deliberately at being a mother. I started my blog, *Dare to Dream,* to encourage women to dream. I became involved in public affairs for my church, which included launching the Know Your Neighbor website, meant to encourage members of my church to be more civic-minded. Through that initiative I became acquainted with Clayton and Matt Christensen, with whom I would eventually establish the investment firm Rose Park Advisors.

In 2007, I also realized it wasn't time for me to leave Wall Street, but rather to step into a different role. Sometimes when we leave one thing, we want to leave it completely. Yet I had spent fifteen years working very, very hard to become a competent analyst. Was it really logical that none of that would matter as I dreamed my next dream? The answer was no. So even as I blogged, and wrote yet another business proposal that didn't quite work, I gradually moved into one of my current dreams, cofounding an investment firm. Where I am today is a very different place than where I thought I was going when I left Merrill Lynch. Yet it's a much more logical dream, one that builds on my various strengths, innate talents, and acquired competencies.

Sometimes we need to jumpstart our discoveries. One tool for calculating next steps is to make a list of people we admire, and to interview them. Sometimes an actual interview is possible, often it isn't. It doesn't matter. As we formulate the questions we would ask, we clarify what we need to know. In asking, we can discover our next steps. This is exactly what Janika Dillon (see chapter 6) did when she began to explore the possibility of pursuing a PhD in history. She made a list of questions she had, and then was fortunate to interview Harvard University history professor Laurel Thatcher Ulrich. In addition to winning a Pulitzer Prize for *A Midwife's Tale* and authoring *Well-Behaved Women Seldom Make History*, Ulrich has also managed to rear five children.

Janika Dillon: *An Interview with One of My Heroes*

JANIKA DILLON: Your life's work has been to study the daily lives of women in history. What do you think is the benefit to women today in looking back?

LAUREL ULRICH: The biggest benefit is exemplified by author Christine de Pizan, who wrote in 1405, in The Book of the City of Ladies, "There is nothing in the world that women can't do."

There's a classic narrative that "Women have been confined to the home and then maybe twenty years ago there was a woman's movement and all these opportunities opened up. Or conversely, all these terrible things started to happen," depending on your point of view. What we learn from Christine's book is the variety of things women have been: inventors, leaders, gardeners, religious heroines, and queens. If you look at the long view, women have always contributed to the economy of their society—always!

DILLON: What were some of the obstacles you faced in becoming the kind of writer you wanted to become?

ULRICH: Time. Finding time to write and forcing myself to use the small amounts of time that I had. When I was doing Beginner's Boston, a guide to the Boston area, when my kids went down for a nap, I had to choose between trying to write and taking a nap myself. It was a hard choice.

I continue to face this same challenge every day of my life. Shall I sit down and be miserable for a little while until I can make it work or not? Writing is very, very hard for me, and it has to happen daily. It's hard to produce more than one paragraph a day. Sometimes I let my students see my really rotten initial drafts. It's comforting for them to realize, "Oh, she has trouble, too!"

DILLON: Who helped you along this path and what kind of help did you need?

ULRICH: The number-one help and support has been my husband. He often recognized better than I did what really made me happy. He was also a great practical help by doing his share with the children and he had a good income. Let's face it. That helped. I didn't have to work for money. My first paying job was when I was in my forties.

Second to my husband was my network of Latter-Day Saint women in the greater Boston area and New Hampshire: they believed in me.

DILLON: So, how did your kids fit into the picture?

ULRICH: I did my graduate degrees one course at a time. My oldest was in elementary school when I began and he was in college when I finished. I got my bachelor's degree in 1960, my master's degree in 1971, and my PhD in 1980, when I was forty-two. My oldest child is fifteen years older than my youngest. My kids were good sports. They grew up with me boiling things over, destroying pots; they joke about my absentmindedness.

DILLON: Did you ever dream you'd go from a small-town Idaho girl to Pulitzer Prize–winning author and professor at Harvard? What advice might you have for women pursuing their dreams?

ULRICH: Well, first, no. I never imagined that I'd be doing the kind of work I'm doing now or be in the place I'm now in. So, I didn't plan my life. The advice I'd give people is that old cliché, "Bloom where you're planted." Do whatever you do wholeheartedly and with joy: the joy really is in the doing. I don't think we can expect or plan or attempt to win the prizes. What I attempted to do was write with passion and in a way that would be accessible to other people. I didn't ever want to just write books for other historians.

I really didn't think I had achieved that accessibility with *A Midwife's Tale*, so it was a surprise to me that it had the kind of success it did. But the book was a joy to do. It was a transforming experience, really. The fifteen minutes of fame are exciting, but that's not what sustains any of us. If you don't enjoy the small pieces of whatever it is that your job is, you're probably not going to enjoy the end product when you get there. The best predictor of happiness in the future is, in fact, enjoying what you are doing right now.

There are so many nuggets here for any of us looking to pursue our dreams. Laurel Ulrich loved to write. She loved history, and she discovered her way to her dream over several decades. To illustrate my point about how our questions point us toward next steps, let's restate what Janika Dillon asked Laurel Ulrich:

- What obstacles will I face in becoming the writer I want to become? (i.e., What obstacles will I face in achieving my dream?)
- Who can I count on to support me?
- What kind of help might I need as I pursue this possibility?
- How do I balance attending to others and to myself?

Dillon was able to interview someone she greatly admires. It's unlikely that many of us will be able to do the same. Still, there's enormous value in simply knowing whom we admire, and what we'd ask him or her. When we admire someone, it's almost always because we see a piece of ourselves mirrored in that person. If we will articulate what we admire and what we'd like to learn from that person, we are in effect saying, "This is a piece of my 'self' I want to develop, that I have in me to develop. My gut tells me that you—person-I-admire—hold some clues."

As we move through our process of discovery, let's again consider Psyche's first task: the sorting of the seeds. There's another ancient story, an allegory really, from a prophet named Alma that teaches how we can know which seeds are good seeds (or in the parlance of this book, which dreams are the right ones for us), and which steps are the right steps to take toward our dream. First, we have to plant the seed. This is an *a priori* assumption. We do have to dabble in some dreams, but once we begin to dabble, we can know if that dream and the course we are pursuing to achieve that dream makes sense because:

1. The dream enlarges our soul. The right dreams are those that bind us to those we love. As a result, they will feel good.
2. This dream enlightens our minds. When it's the right dream for us, ideas will begin to flow. This happens differently for everyone, but I know when an idea is a good one because I start to see doors to more and more possibilities opening in my mind. When it's not a good idea, the possibilities aren't there.
3. If a dream feels right in both our heart and head, the dream becomes delicious. I love that word: *delicious*. A good dream is one that expands our hearts and enlightens our minds. It's pleasing and delightful, and, like planting a seed, exploring a dream is a process of growing and transforming; reaping a delicious harvest (finding joy) is the result of finding and pursuing the right dreams.

OPENING OURSELVES TO SERENDIPITY

When we are open to the process of discovering how to achieve our dreams, we open ourselves to serendipity, as photographer Saydi Shumway (saydiphotography.blogspot.com), a mother who also holds a bachelor's degree from Wellesley college and a master's degree in social work from Columbia University, found.

Saydi Shumway: *The Snapshot That Changed My Life*

I expected I'd go to college, maybe attend graduate school, and then get married, work for a while, and have kids. That all happened. Perhaps not in the same way or as quickly as I thought it would, but it happened. What happened after that was unexpected.

I had my first two children just sixteen months apart, by choice. My thought was, I'm devoting my life to this motherhood career right now, might as well pack it in, like I do with everything else. It seemed to be a sensible plan, but living through that plan has been harder than I had anticipated.

I thought the first eighteen months with two small children would be killer, but after that, things would get better. But even when my second child was well over two years old I felt far from having things under control. I didn't see myself as the mom I'd always wanted to be. I had envisioned myself cheerfully discovering life with my kids: devouring books with them, taking them out to bask in the wonders of nature, crafting, cooking, and helping others. I thought I'd be that cool mom who enjoys spontaneity but also runs a tight ship, teaching my kids to be polite, make good decisions, be obedient, and to work hard.

The reality was that I was tired and disorganized most of the time. I didn't have a structured discipline strategy. I "lost it" more often than I'd like to admit, and I could barely get through the piles of laundry, let alone take that weekly trip to the library. Instead, I made a monthly library trip, mostly to lug back an ambitious bagful of unread, overdue books.

Around that time a dear friend snapped a picture of my son Charlie and me at the beach. She e-mailed it to me and I printed it out. I looked at it, and looked at it, and looked at it. Because after I got past how I didn't like my hair and my nose (sometimes that's all we see in pictures of ourselves), I saw for the first time the beautiful, authentic reality of my mothering revealed in the image.

Looking in on that scene felt vastly different from living it. The image did not present the haggard, disorganized failure of a mother I had felt I was at points throughout that day, week, and month. Instead, this photograph depicted a happy, fulfilled mom, one who was drinking in her delighted little boy sitting securely on her lap. This photograph had captured the tiny bit of perfection that exists in my life.

I subsequently put the photograph on my refrigerator so I could look at it every day to remind me that I do love mothering—and perhaps more importantly, because I treasure this tangible representation of the mom I want to be, and how I want my kids to feel: comfortable, happy, secure, and delighted.

The thirteenth-century German philosopher Meister Eckhart said, "When the soul wishes to experience something, she throws an image of the experience out before her and enters into her own image." The picture of Charlie and me on the beach is the image that my soul wants to experience.

I've always enjoyed photography, but it wasn't until the epiphany with a particular photograph that I realized how powerful photography can be. I started taking my camera to work with me so I could take pictures of my social work clients while they interacted with their babies. I was amazed to see that these photos did the same thing for them that the beach snapshot did for me.

These images have also changed my philosophy as a photographer. I now view photography as a tool to reveal emotion and connections, one that captures true pieces of relationships, rather than just the right smile or pose. I hope my work helps people create images that their souls long to experience. Images so tangible they can jump right in and be the person they want to be.

In her head, Saydi felt like her dream of ideal motherhood wasn't happening, but through the serendipity of a casual photo snapped and shared by a friend, she experienced a new vision of her dream. Her new vision then helped Saydi share the power of photography with others, influencing the way those women engage in their own dreams of motherhood. If we are open to serendipity, we may find that our dreams are shaped, molded, and changed by these seemingly random moments of discovery.

DREAMING AND DISCOVERING

Conventional planning, at which many of us excel, will hold us in good stead as we dream, but dreaming is ultimately about feeling our way toward what we were meant to do. As we embark on the process of discovery, the odds are very high that the dreams we think we want or need to pursue will be very different from what we actually pursue. Similarly, the means for achieving those dreams will be different than anticipated. As we seek to discover our dreams, interviewing people who have done what we think we want to do can be a way to jumpstart the process.

As we experiment and sort through different possibilities (that is, make mistakes), we discover whether we want to stay the course or move in a different direction. As with the planting of seeds, when we hit upon the right dreams for us they will become delicious.

SIFTING, SORTING, SOWING...

- In what areas of your life does conventional planning work?
- In which areas do you find discovery-driven planning is most effective?
- What one or two small things—that can be done in one or two hours time—can you do right now that will move you toward a dream? After you do them, what do you know that you didn't know before? (Keep in mind that you may learn more if something hasn't turned out as you expected than if it has.)
- If you were to interview someone you admire, or someone who has accomplished some piece of what you want to accomplish, what questions would you ask?

When the soul wishes to experience something, she throws an image of the experience out before her and enters into her own image.
　　　　　　　—Meister Eckhart, thirteenth-century philosopher

- Have you considered taking a photograph of what it is you want to achieve? (You can also clip photographs or images that represent your goal.)
- As you pursue a dream, is the pursuit binding you to those you love?
- Are the steps you are taking—and the dream itself—delicious? If so, keep going, and allocate more time to those ideas and that path. If not, then reevaluate and look to pivot.

12

CREATE YOUR DARE
TO DREAM TEAM

Not long ago, I had one of those days when I cried, and I cried, and then I cried some more. I was so heartbroken that, apart from the meltdown to which my husband was privy, I wanted to avoid contact with anyone I knew and sought refuge at a nearby bookstore. Wanting some comfort, I sent an e-mail to a friend outlining what had happened, and she immediately tried to call me. I didn't initially pick up, but she persisted. I finally summoned the courage to answer the phone. Yes, courage. Because I was afraid that in recounting my experience I would again unravel, appearing needy and vulnerable.

In *The Price of Privilege*, author Madeline Levine titles a chapter "Having Everything Except What We Need Most: The Isolation of Affluent Moms." She writes, "Experienced clinicians find an unexpectedly high amount of depression, anxiety, loneliness, and plain old unhappiness among well-to-do mothers." Levine concludes that affluent moms can be many things: bright, competitive, persistent, protective, interesting, and funny. But they are not vulnerable, at least not publicly. Vulnerability is a kind of admission of hurt feelings, of neediness, of sadness, of things not going well.

As my friend and I spoke, I shared how sad I was. After listening for about ten minutes, she said something akin to, "That's really hard." No profound words of wisdom were asked for, needed, or even wanted, but because she listened and I knew that she cared, I felt better.

EXPERIENCING SYSTERGY

In an article titled "UCLA Study on Friendship Among Women," author Gale Berkowitz writes "women respond to stress with a cascade of brain chemicals, the hormone oxytocin in particular, that cause us to make and maintain friendships with other women. When we actually engage in befriending, more oxytocin is released, which further counters stress and produces a calming effect."

If our sisterhood can buoy us up on a bad day simply because of how we are hardwired, just think of the possibilities that this feel-good hormone releases as we share our dreams and experience the positive stress that comes as we pursue those dreams. Doing our dreams will require us to be vulnerable, which is one of the most frightening places any of us can go, but when we do, we'll cross a bridge to a happier place. I describe this process of supporting and enabling the dreams of others as *systergy*. For Stephanie Soper, a former education consultant for the State Department's Office of Overseas Schools, who now does intuitively guided emotional healing, systergy was crucial to overcoming her painter's block.

Stephanie Soper: *Portrait of an Artist*

After nearly fifteen years of avoidance, I've decided I want to start painting again. I've watched my friend Janna Taylor's dreams (and her accompanying fears) unfold over the last two years. It has been thrilling to watch her daring, but I wasn't sure I had the nerve to do the same. In addition to Janna, two other friends, Jan and Michaela, have steadily "noodged" me back to painting. They, themselves, have been dancing around their own dreams of becoming published writers. Both are so gifted that it seems ridiculous to even imagine that they might not succeed. But I also know how natural it can be to sabotage one's own goals.

A few weeks ago, while Michaela and I were on the phone telling each other yet again that we *really should* paint/write, we simultaneously had a "feeling" that we should promise each other to write (her) and paint (me) for three hours a week and report on our work Thursday afternoon. Miraculously, making a commitment to one another has worked; we have checked in with each other four weeks in a row. She has a story nearly finished, and I've completed one new painting, finished three that have been half-done for forever, and started a new one. It's been about more than painting and writing, though—it's been about figuring out our fears and stepping through them.

I finally finished a painting that publicly displayed my grief over not having had children. I don't know which was harder, finishing the painting or acknowledging my grief. This painting was of a forest along the banks of a river. I knew it was missing something, but didn't know what. A year ago, I figured out the missing element: little ghost babies; the five babies I'd always wanted; the river was a River of Tears of Grief. I couldn't make myself paint those babies until last week; finishing this painting has been surprisingly liberating.

It was done in the medium I'm most comfortable with, temperas. Tempera paint (the poster paint we used in kindergarten) has saturated, brilliant, opaque color. It's cheap and it dries quickly, so you get quick satisfaction.

But the real reason I use temperas is to avoid oils. Using oils meant a real commitment to painting; it meant saying I am an artist, not just that I do a little painting, and I have avoided that.

A decade ago, I bought a gorgeous collection of oil paint tubes, a palette, brushes, and turpenoid. They went untouched until today. I had to wrench the caps with pliers to get them unstuck (kind of metaphor, I guess). I half hoped they were too dried out to use, but alas, they were still fresh and I had no excuse.

I did a so-so job painting today. Surprisingly, I am willing to keep trying. For a perfectionist eldest daughter who is used to success, this is a titanic shift in perspective. The *dare* part of *dare to dream* came alive. Well into my work on one canvas I decided it was too big. I had made a wrong choice, which wasn't a big deal (but allowing myself to think it wasn't a big deal *was* a big deal).

I began again on a smaller canvas and made a fresher-looking drawing. It looks like a sailboat far from the shore, but it represents my capacity and willingness to sail in deep emotional waters, to become my whole self.

I'm okay that the painting isn't perfect.

Okay that I'm doing something that I really want to do, even though I'm not very good at it, and that after all the work that lies ahead, I may still not like it.

Okay to have to learn instead of starting out as an expert.

For me, this takes daring.

Stephanie has experienced firsthand the importance of women daring and then mentoring one another as we dream. As a child, Stephanie's three dreams were to be telepathic, be an artist, and be a doctor. Though she's not a medical doctor, she does help people heal. Because she is painting again—largely due to encouragement from her friends—she is living out all three of her dreams.

Few of us dream well on our own, and women in particular find it difficult, because the skills we bring to any enterprise are so often overlooked or undervalued; this is why we need a Dare to Dream team. Our team might include friends, but more than likely it will consist of friends of friends, or contacts of contacts, or people we meet serendipitously. Importantly, the team is separate from those who love us and encourage us; these are people who know *how to do* what we want to do.

REACHING OUT TO STRANGERS OF CONSEQUENCE

In *Consequential Strangers*, authors Melinda Blau and Karen Fingerman write about the importance of people who don't seem to matter but really do, as they "bring novelty and information into our lives, allow us to exercise different parts of ourselves, and open up new opportunities." To illustrate that point, the authors cite research about a group of African American women in an impoverished neighborhood: "These savvy mothers were not merely conscientious or strict, they had strong family support from sisters, aunts, and extended kin. [They] were also adept at community bridging. They used church members and others outside their immediate environment to get their children into libraries, admitted to parochial or magnet schools, involved in after-school programs, scouting, or other organizations that bettered their lives."

Securing better opportunities for children sounds like a dream to me, and consequential strangers facilitated this dream. Consider this passage from Blau and Fingerman:

> Social network analysts and scientists who map and measure the patterns and flows of relationships agree that most of us like to think of ourselves as independent agents, marching through life to our own iPod soundtrack, but our relationships propel us as well. The problem is that networks are like traffic jams. You can easily see the cars that surround you, your intimates. But it takes a helicopter to view your entire entourage—your social convoy.... A handful of people travel alongside you for miles. The peripheral people, neither family nor close friends, your consequential strangers are often there for a particular segment of the trip and tend to serve specific needs.
>
> Our convoys represent our history and our potential. Seeing our lives from this aerial view allows us to better understand the situations we're in, the decisions we make, and the way we solve problems.... In short, life is as much a function of whom you associate with as who you are, and the ability to bring people into your convoy when you need them is a key coping mechanism in a complex world.

Consequential strangers were key to me achieving my dream of a career. One "stranger" in particular was Jim Cowles, a senior banker and de facto boss at Smith Barney. When I was pregnant with my first child (David, now fifteen), my boss wanted to fire me because he knew that I knew he wasn't very competent. He would have, had my performance not been stellar. Enter Jim Cowles. I didn't know him well and still don't, but for a few brief months, he became a part of my convoy, involving me in special projects until I went on maternity leave. When I returned, he brokered my move into equity research, which for me was a career-defining move.

Within the *Dare to Dream* community, many strangers are of consequence. In early 2009, Elizabeth Harmer Dionne recommended that Saren Eyre Loosli (Saren and Elizabeth were classmates at Wellesley) and I connect and that she write a guest post for my blog; during the back-and-forth, we developed a rapport. Saren and business partner April Perry subsequently asked if I would join the Power of Moms advisory board. Saren and April dream of connecting hundreds of thousands of mothers to one another. By expanding their social convoy to include people they didn't know, or at least didn't know well, they are propelling their dream forward.

ARTICULATING WHAT WE WANT

Another important element of connecting with consequential strangers is being clear on what it is we want to accomplish. It would seem to go without saying, but given how much most of us struggle to articulate what it is we dream of doing, I want to underscore the importance of saying out loud what we want. That is what Stephanie Dahl, who has a master's degree in early childhood education, did as she dreamed of becoming a mother. You can read more at *A Lovely Problem to Have* (alovelyproblemtohave.blogspot.com.)

Stephanie Dahl: *Say It Out Loud*

As a child, I wasn't obsessed with the idea of becoming a mom. It was just a natural progression in the sequence of events that was to come. I would go to college, get married, and then become a mother. My husband and I tried to conceive for several years, utilizing both the "wait-and-see" and "doctor-please-help-us" approaches. Neither method worked, not even once.

To someone with typical fertility, the concept of infertility might be challenging to understand. I wanted to be a mother, but I was unable to conceive; I felt "less than"—less than a woman, less than a wife. More than anything else, I wanted to be a mother. We came to a point in treatment where the next recommended course of action was in vitro fertilization. The pursuit of biological children seemed selfish and futile at that point, as we knew there are literally thousands upon thousands of children, born and unborn, local and international, who need families. We began to pursue adoption. In doing so, I gave voice to my dream of becoming a mother.

- I mentioned my dream to the ob-gyn who visited me prior to a surgery I had to remove a suspicious growth on my ovary.
- I made an announcement at work.
- I started a website. The adoption process requires a great deal of paperwork, so the website gave me the opportunity to express my desire even more.
- I discussed my dream with the physician who performed my pre-adoption physical exam, performed to ensure my physical fitness.
- I discussed my dream with the social worker as she evaluated my home and my mental fitness.

- I discussed my dream with our pastor, who needed to testify to the adoption agency about my "spiritual fitness."

The question became not "Would I become a mother?" but "When?" We were told to expect to wait a year, although it could easily be longer. However, two weeks after completing our adoption paperwork and prerequisites, a potential birth mother chose us and our daughter was born. We brought her home from the hospital when she was three days old. We cuddled her and rocked her, sang to her, and smiled at her. I wiped away tears of joy. When she was four weeks old, we found out that we were expecting. Eight months later, I gave birth to a healthy baby girl.

I now have two daughters, nine months apart.

People often have theories about why we could suddenly conceive after adopting. Some say the mommy hormones were at work. Others say I probably just relaxed. I'm not certain, but I do know that if I had not verbalized my hope of becoming a mother, it would never have happened. Our voices, our declarations, are verbal anointments of our intentions and desires. Through spoken words, our prayers begin life in the physical realm.

Stephanie learned that an important part of making our dreams happen is having the courage to articulate what it is we want. When we speak our dreams aloud, we invite potential consequential strangers to aid our cause and even become part of our Dare to Dream team.

MAKING CONNECTIONS FOR EACH OTHER

As mentioned in chapter 3, Psyche's third seemingly impossible task is to fill a flask from an inhospitable stream etched into a jagged cliff that is guarded by dragons. Instead of risking her life, she convinces Zeus' eagle to swoop down, fill the flask, and soar back up to safety.

To make our dreams happen, we sometimes need an eagle, an eagle who has skills, connections, or knowledge that we need but don't currently have; often, this eagle is not someone we know directly. Because as women we are adept at relationships and we know how to bootstrap, we can get to the expertise we need, even if it seems at first to be out of our reach. It may be harder for us if what we want to accomplish requires that we go outside of traditional women's networks, but we can. Each of us has a social network or entourage. We know people who know people who know people. Each of us is in a position to open doors of possibility for others. Some people do this better than others. When someone is willing to bridge us into their world, they are giving us a gift. Consider *The Lion, the Witch, and the Wardrobe*. When Lucy opens the door into the magical world of Narnia, she invites her siblings into the world. We all have this type of opportunity and privilege.

ACKNOWLEDGING AND RECIPROCATING

Once people are willing to travel with our convoy for a time, it's vital that we reciprocate. At the very least, we must acknowledge and give credit to those who help us, and/or we must pay it forward. Commenting on Dante's *Inferno*, T.S. Eliot recognized the importance of reciprocity when he stated, "Hell is a place where nothing connects with nothing." When we reciprocate, we forge a connection.

In addition to the dozens of women who have contributed their stories, two women in particular have comprised *my* pre-publisher dream team for the book you now hold in your hands: Amy Jameson assisted me with conceptual edits of my drafts and Melissa Stanton fine-tuned my message with her detailed line editing. In analyzing the dynamic of my relationships with my own Dare to Dream teams, I've made some broadly applicable observations:

1. **Start with short-term projects:** If you intend to start a business or a nonprofit, before expanding the scope of the relationship, work on a short-term project first, such as a benefit for the community or your children's school. Lamentably, I don't always do this. I have at times moved impetuously into a major project without vetting my partner(s) and they me. In time, we discover that we can't work together because we have different timetables, different visions, and different views on the give versus get, and things have gotten dicey. I offer this advice to you as a poorer but much wiser girl.

2. **Trust our collaborators' competence:** Once we've worked on a few limited-scope projects and have fully worked out the rules of engagement, it's important to trust our collaborators. If we're micromanaging, we may just need to stop. Or maybe we didn't choose our partners as well as we thought we did. For example, after I broadly outlined for graphic designer Brandon Jameson (Amy's husband) what I wanted for the Dare to Dream logo, he came back with something completely different than what I expected, which, I must admit, I didn't really like. Because I'd loved his previous work, I was willing to "live with" his vision for a few days, and I came to realize that his vision was perfect, just perfect! The logo visually

communicated that *when women put their heads together, they experience systergy and can accomplish their dreams.*

3. **Recognize that our collaborators will not be good at what we do well:** If we choose someone for a project because they can do what we can't (web design, photography, accounting), the almost-certain corollary is that we will be good at things they aren't. When we can harness "smart in different ways," we have the makings of a Dare to Dream team.

4. **Give others their due in terms of compensation and credit:** When our collaborators do good work, give them credit. Pay them if the transaction is for-profit and whether for profit or not, tell as many people as possible what good work that person does. Because someone doesn't ask for praise or compensation doesn't mean he or she doesn't want or even need it. Many people don't know how to ask, or even know what their skills are worth. What a gift we can give if we help friends and coworkers know their worth.

A member of my dream team, Amy Jameson (aplusbworks .com), a stay-at-home mother and a part-time literary agent and freelance editor, learned the importance of consequential strangers at a critical moment in her dreaming, and later took the opportunity to help another stranger achieve her dreams.

Amy Jameson: *Dream It Forward*

When I moved to New York City at age twenty-three, I had no idea what I wanted to do, but shortly after arriving I landed a job as an assistant at a literary agency. I didn't know what a literary agent was when I started. Now, twelve years later, I am a literary agent with my own independent business. I act on behalf of authors, helping place their manuscripts with a publisher, negotiating their contracts, smoothing things over when feathers get ruffled, acting as cheerleader, therapist, and advisor.

After six years at the New York agency, working my way up from my original job as an assistant, I was promoted to a "junior agent" role. When I first joined the firm I had been told that secretaries are secretaries and agents are agents and "we don't promote from within." Granted, I still mostly served the needs of other agents' clients, but I was doing everything that the other agents did. Unfortunately, despite my years of hard work, I consistently felt snubbed and overlooked by those in charge.

After years of fantasizing about leaving the agency and going out on my own, the decision was made for me. I was suddenly let go. At the time, I felt the floor had opened up beneath me. But losing my job was the best possible thing that could have happened to me there. I did need to move on, and since I didn't have the courage to do it myself, the universe gave me a shove in the right direction.

The timing was impeccable. A few weeks later, I found out I was pregnant with my first child. During this time, I had lunch with another agent, a friend of a friend. Her story mirrored my own. She had been at a big agency for many years, where she felt underappreciated and overlooked. She had recently left to set up her own shop.

That lunch was a turning point for me. I had dreamed of being on my own, but hearing this woman's story and her advice gave me the confidence to believe I could actually make it happen. I would count my lunch companion as an essential member of my "Dare to Dream team," even though she remains a casual acquaintance. She gave me exactly what I needed when I needed it. Many others encouraged my dream.

My husband, Brandon, was and is probably the most important person on my dream team. He has supported my dream in countless ways: as my business partner, my technical advisor, my in-house graphic designer/webmaster, my listening ear, and my shoulder to cry on. I also had supportive clients who bravely left the safety of an established agency to follow me into uncharted waters. Without them, my dream would have been impossible to achieve.

I recently made a very deliberate decision to become a member of someone else's dream team. An acquaintance asked if I might take on one of his students, who aspired to be a literary agent, as an intern. I had just had my third child and was overwhelmed with juggling many responsibilities. The timing was not good.

But I agreed to have lunch with his student, Terri, wondering what I was getting myself into. Her story really touched me. Terri is a single mom of four children, now all grown, and she had missed an earlier opportunity to pursue a career as a literary agent because of the necessity of providing for her family. She was again pursuing her bachelor's degree in English, a degree that was interrupted by the demands of motherhood. Terri explained that many years ago, when she caught the vision of what a literary agent does, she realized that helping someone else get their work published was even more exciting, more satisfying, than seeing her own work published. That struck me. I could have said the same. I felt inspired to help Terri make her dream come true, and I offered her the opportunity to intern with me. Only Terri can really make her dream happen, but I'm excited to help her acquire some of the tools she will need along the way.

We dream best when we dream together, but sometimes the assemblage of people that will form our Dare to Dream team are not quite within reach. That is one purpose of my *Dare to Dream* blog and the community that is being built around it. The *Dare to Dream* website serves as a place for consequential strangers to meet and share encouragement, advice, and resources.

In time, my dream is for the *Dare to Dream* community to proffer not just encouragement and the bartering of expertise, but to eventually have the capital (i.e., cash) to invest in one another's dreams. Paraphrasing economist John Maynard Keynes, we must have the courage to take limited means, and to invest in and encourage others. Chrysula Winegar (see chapter 2) once described me as an "investor in stocks, people, concepts, and dreams." I think she's quite accurate about what I aspire to be. I want to invest in people's dreams through my words, my expertise, my connections, and, eventually, my capital as a venture capitalist. This is my dream. And I'm saying it out loud.

TAKING STOCK IN ONE ANOTHER...

Our convoys represent our history and our potential.
—Melinda Blau and Karen Fingerman,
authors of *Consequential Strangers*

- Business philosopher Jim Rohn wrote, "You are the sum of the five people that you spend the most time with." As you dream, are you surrounding yourself with artists of encouragement, facilitators of dreams?
- What Dare to Dream project are you working on or thinking of undertaking? Do you have a Dare to Dream team?
- "Through spoken words, our prayers begin life in the physical realm," wrote blogger Stephanie Dahl. What do you need to say aloud so you can begin to assemble your dream team?

- Are consequential strangers helping you make your dream happen? If so, how did you find them?
- Are we adequately compensating people for the work they do, whether via money or barter? And if they say, "You don't need to pay me," are we insisting on some form of recompense, especially with other women?
- Who are you investing in? On whose Dare to Dream team do you serve?
- To what extent are we, as parents, part of our children's Dare to Dream team? Do we collaborate with them and trust their strengths but avoid micromanaging?

13

LEARN TO BOOTSTRAP

After my first year of college, my mom announced she was out of money. It wasn't what I wanted to hear, but tough luck. I went home, got a job as a girl Friday at Priam, a Silicon Valley–based corporation, and saved what I earned. A year later I returned to college, knowing something I hadn't known when I left: I may need to make my own way in life to get what I want, and I can.

During economic downturns, many of us face similar circumstances. In trudging through a gloom-and-doom atmosphere, there are things we want to do for ourselves or our family, businesses we want to expand or start, but can't.

Here's the reality: whether times are good or bad, many of us don't have what we want, or what we perceive we "need," to pursue our dreams. In 2007, *Entrepreneur* magazine and the Corporate Research Board screened ninety-five thousand companies to compile "The Hot 500 Fastest Growing Businesses in America." Only 28 percent of those companies had access to bank loans or lines of credit, while just 18 percent were funded by private investors, and a mere 3.5 percent received funding from venture capitalists. In other words, more than half of the companies on the list were growing and thriving despite having limited access to the funds most people would deem necessary to nurture a business.

LEVERAGING CURRENT ASSETS

Making our dreams happen is about leveraging the skills, money, and time we already have. It's about starting where we are and avoiding the lottery mentality:

- If only I had a larger home, I'd be more organized.
- If only I had a housekeeper, I would be a really great mother.
- If only I had a fairy godmother like Oprah, my nonprofit would take off.
- If only I had an investor to finance me, I could start my business.

Marathoner and mother of five Emily Orton (see chapter 1) said it well: "A budget of money, time, or space shouldn't be about what we can't do or have, but how to make it happen." No doubt many of the entrepreneurs behind the "Hot 500" companies sought funding, but it just wasn't available. So they started anyway, perhaps because their reality was "Do, or Don't Eat," and they were thus highly incentivized to make their businesses work. Their determination to succeed was strong enough that 61 percent of the entrepreneurs turned a profit within a year.

Dana King, a St. Louis-based interior designer whose mission is to "make good design happen for everyone," is a terrific example of an entrepreneur who focuses not on what she doesn't have, but on how to make her dream happen. When a pitch she made to HGTV for its *Next Design Star* reality show was rejected, she decided to try her hand at filming her own show. Her hurdles: limited financial resources and very limited technical know-how. (You can follow Dana's progress and her dream at seedanado.com.)

Dana King: *Geekifying Myself*

Computers—I affectionately call them "confusers"—and I have a long love-hate relationship. The hardware is too hard. The software is too soft. I have been waiting for a computer that is *juuuuuuust* right, and doesn't require an advanced degree to install or special geek aptitude to operate.

Ahh, the iPhone. It changed my life overnight.

Now I can interact with a digital device intelligently and confidently. Thank you, Steve Jobs, the only geek, besides my husband, Dan, that I've been madly in love with. My iPhone makes me feel empowered.

For more than twenty years, I have been reliant on Dan to help me operate most electronic devices, and our marriage has been on the edge at times because of my digital codependence. Our biggest arguments have been over my disinterest, distrust, and general dislike of digital devices that don't read my mind and automatically know what I want them to do.

Since the Dell won't talk to me, I took my frustration out on Dan. These days, if you sleep, you get left behind in the cybergalactic fog of blogging, linking, Twittering, and Facebooking in a way that can be detrimental to your hopes and dreams.

You learn what you want to learn. I just didn't want to learn to use technology. But I do want to succeed. I want to be a media mogul, just like Rachael Ray and Oprah. I desire a media platform to teach and spread my gospel about celebrating creative living. The application and audition tape I sent to HGTV went unnoticed. To heck with the studio. I just need a camera guy or gal and an editor; maybe a producer, too; and some big bucks, or sponsors. I've got none of those. Does that mean the dream dies?

Dan woke me up one morning with, "I think you should start a vlog."

"I have a blog," I reminded him.

"No a *VVVVVVVlog*," he repeated. "Post video of what you do. You don't need a camera crew or sponsors. You just need a flip camera. You can edit the footage yourself."

Dan knows better than to encourage my projects because he is certain to become collateral damage. I took this suggestion to mean he must believe in me. He must really love me. Encouraging me to embrace a digital project is like asking for a tornado to land on our house.

Dan convinced me that vlogging would be easy, if I would just take the time to learn and stop whining. So I took the challenge, and I reserved the right to whine. Except that he was right. Editing video is easier than I thought. In no time (about twenty hours) I produced my first short film (we're talking seven power-packed minutes), complete with music and captions. I can now host, film, edit, and produce a show. Who knew?

My vlog has since turned into a website portfolio that has received the attention of a local television show producer. A local production company asked to film my design club—a concept I promote via my postings—and produced a promotional video for me free of charge. If pictures paint a thousand words, video tells even more. In other words, it's far easier to show you who I am than to tell you.

I still get frustrated, but I tell myself it's nothing that a little time can't remedy. And in time, I will *geekify* myself for my betterment, and for my dreams. As Apple's Steve Jobs, and my Dan, have shown me, geeks can rock the world!

With the experience of starting her vlog, I asked Dana about the process of bootstrapping her way to her own television show. Here are two pointers from Dana:

Start by doing what you can do: "I couldn't afford the best camera or a camera crew and editors, so I just use my flip camera and point it at myself. I'm finding that people like the artsy rawness of the videos. What I thought was a limitation has become an asset."

Let others join in: "Standing outside the Goodwill, I was filming myself for a piece on thrift store shopping. A gentleman on his way in offered to tape me. He didn't ask why or what I was doing, but he noticed the fun I was having and wanted to join in. I have these experiences regularly. I wonder how I will film something myself, but then help comes along. My limitations actually make the experience fun."

TURNING SCARCITY INTO OPPORTUNITY

Dana has a dream of having a media platform. She thought she didn't have the resources, but she soon recognized that she did, in fact, have enough to start. In late 2008, one of my business partners, Clayton Christensen offered his opinion that the recession would have an "unmitigated positive impact on innovation" because "when the tension is greatest and resources are most limited, people are actually a lot more open to rethinking the fundamental way they do business." This theory is supported by the Kaufmann Foundation statistic that "51 percent of the Fortune 500 companies began during a recession or bear market or both."

Whether launching a business or pursuing a dream, there

are many high-profile instances in which a lack of resources ultimately proved to be a boon, rather than a bane. If we dig a bit, each of us can uncover examples among friends and family, and ourselves. Would most children have as many opportunities as they do in sports, music, or other extracurricular activities without parents, mothers in particular, who are accomplished at bartering as a way to stretch limited family budgets? Would kids have as many chances to explore their interests if their parents weren't so adept at arranging for carpooling, chaperoning, and borrowing, thus enabling their kids to participate? Without the constraints of time, money, and health, would the online retailer Shabby Apple exist? (For a reminder of how that business came to be, see chapter 5.) If my parents could have paid for college, would I have caught an early glimpse of corporate life during the Silicon Valley heyday? Would I have ever set foot on Wall Street had I not needed to work to put my husband through school?

All of us have had the opportunity to bootstrap if we look hard enough. Men seem to know how to do this in the business world: 88 percent of the founders of *Entrepreneur* magazine's Hot 500 were men. But I wonder if women aren't better at bootstrapping than we think we are. Chronically under resourced (whether due to the gender pay gap or ceding our resources to conform to societal expectations), women continually feel the tension of having too little budget and too little time. Because of this tension, we are expert at rethinking how to get things done. Many of us know how to turn scarcity into opportunity.

Recall Psyche's second task, in which Aphrodite requires her to obtain fleece from the rams of the sun. On the advice of the reeds on the river's edge, she waits until sundown to pick the fleece from brambles the rams have brushed against. This, to me, is a great example of starting with very little and still being able to get the job done, and without putting oneself at risk. We can do the same by starting with what we have, without putting too many of our resources at risk, as we discover our way to achieving our dream. You'll marvel at what you can accomplish from small beginnings. This is important because it allows us to focus on what we *can* do instead of fretting about our limitations. The next step is to whack away at any residual perfectionism, a major deterrent to achieving our dreams.

SQUARING OFF WITH PERFECTIONISM

As a child, I did so many things well that I could afford to be a perfectionist. In high school, my needing to do things perfectly became problematic. I almost didn't take AP American history. I didn't take calculus or economics because I feared I couldn't get an A. I did get As in the classes I took but, in retrospect, given my chosen career, a B in calculus rather than no calculus at all probably would have been a decent trade. Perfectionism often starts at a young age and can be quite crippling, as Bonnie Tonita White who has worked as a French immersion teacher, public affairs consultant, commercial real estate agent, and retail sales associate, relates in the following story:

Bonnie Tonita White: *Delight in the Doing*

One day, while reading to my toddler Josh, I encouraged him to illustrate the story. This appealed to his creative nature, and he settled in beside me with crayons and paper to draw his interpretation of the tale we'd just read. As Josh began to draw, he became frustrated, and his frustration became a distraction. When I asked what was wrong, he became very agitated and began pounding the crayon onto the paper with forceful, intense strokes. He looked up at me with his big sad eyes and tear-streaked cheeks and said, "It's no good. I can't make it like I see it!" His imagination and past experience with professionally illustrated books exceeded his physical coordination and ability. He had the ability of a three-year-old, with all of the expected glorious crudeness of design, but he wanted the skills of a seasoned illustrator. He sensed his failure and allowed that inadequacy to overcome his desire to draw.

I've recalled this experience many times when disappointed by work that falls short of what I had imagined or envisioned I was capable of achieving. Our imagination fosters a desire to try things. Just because we can't or aren't good at something the first time we try doesn't mean what we are doing has no merit. As I step forward into the next phase of my life, I ask myself: Can I accept the space that lies between my imagination and my best efforts? Or will I stay here safe on this side of my achievements? Can I delight in doing despite the crudeness of my effort as I draw closer to my dreams?

Bonnie's story is one most women can relate to—we have a vision of a grand and glorious dream, but too often a failed first attempt at doing something new keeps us from pursuing that dream. If we cannot accept imperfection along the road to our dreams, we can easily become stuck, "safe on this side of achievements," as Bonnie puts it. And remember that other eyes are watching us: if we quit because our dream isn't perfect, what are we teaching our children?

Learning to bootstrap our way to a dream requires us to do more with less, to get creative to get things done. Perfectionism demands that every detail must be just so, which in many ways is the antithesis of a bootstrapping mentality. Jennifer Thomas holds a bachelors' degree in Italian and art history and pursued graduate studies in art history at the Institute of Fine Arts at NYU. She also is a former fundraiser for MGH Boston; she shares here how she is learning to push perfectionism out of the picture and use the resources she has.

Jennifer Walker Thomas: *King Louis XIV Lives inside My Head*

After years of study in the arts, I have a well-trained eye, and know lovely when I see it. Beauty feeds my soul, but sometimes torments it as well. It turns out that there is an unexpected occupational hazard that comes from a head filled with beautiful things other people conceived of and made; it can be very intimidating to find room in there for your own ideas to generate. Even worse, the trained critic in me is always looking at something with an eye to making it better. So, no matter how hard I have worked at something, I still see only the flaws.

Recently (shortly after returning from a trip to France), I flew into my hometown a few days before a beloved brother's wedding. My parents were hosting his reception in their perfectly lovely backyard, and so there was lots of work to do. I got there early hoping to help, and tackled what was left of my mother's punch list.

I didn't inherit my perfectionism from my mother. She has a very sane, "good enough is good enough" attitude, and is a scientist by training and temperament. So her list was easy enough, but at its end things were pretty far from exquisite. Six hours off the plane I had moved on to a list of my own. I was planting, pruning, painting, and generally moving at a frantic pace. I just kept thinking: "This is David's WEDDING!" I had marshaled the troops and developed an elaborate schedule, but was starting to panic; we didn't have enough time left. Paralysis began to set in. It was at this point that another brother called it as he saw it, and said: "You've got Louis XIV in your head and you've got to kick him out, we've got stuff to do."

He was right, and I have been thinking about that statement ever since. I can remember countless times when I have let Louis and his ilk squelch my dreams. Too often I am paralyzed by both my own sense of the lovely and what others have already accomplished. A garden reception? "Think Versailles!" But, who can possibly live up to that? Perhaps my most painful example of this is the Christmas night I spent crying because my holiday accomplishments hadn't perfectly reflected all my creative ideas. I felt like a failure. My husband was mystified: "How could it possibly have been better?" I let a vision of perfection ruin all my hard work and our peace. That was the real and only failure of the day.

I think that I may have some great dreams inside my head, but the resources at my command are not those of the Sun King. I don't have solitude, or a patron, or a budget, or a staff. I don't even have a desk. I do often have a detailed vision of the end, but am blind when it comes to seeing how it can possibly be achieved or even approximated. So all too often I quit before I start, and Louis conquers.

All this means that my brother was right, and Louis has got to go. I am realizing that if I am ever going to follow a big dream to fruition and create something exquisite of my own, I have got to figure out how to see the ideal, but accept the compromises forced by reality. I have got to somehow stay on speaking terms with perfection but not let that beautiful conversation drown me out. So my resolution this year is to kick Louis out. He can head back to Versailles. It's hard to imagine a better place to live in exile, which has always been exactly my problem.

Jennifer's take is comical, but it does teach us that if we wait for perfection, we may never start. The only real failure is letting the dictates of perfectionism debilitate us, leaving us forever waiting for all the "necessary" resources to arrive before doing our dreams. Bootstrapping teaches us to use what we have, even if it doesn't seem like much, and to begin now.

STARTING WHERE WE ARE

Bootstrapping is about starting where we are with what we have and recognizing that we have so much more on hand than we may think we do. We will likely never have enough of what we think we need, but what we need most is to start. In starting with what we have, we just might be a lot more successful than we would if we waited for outside resources to become available. One of my favorite business mantras is "Patient for growth, impatient for profits." The impatience for profits is about using the resources we have and recognizing that resource-constrained ventures have a track record of success. If we do that first, we can trust that the growth will come.

Bootstrapping is often born out of necessity and requires simply daring to dream that something you want or need is possible. Jolene Edmunds Rockwood who holds an MTS from the Harvard Divinity School wanted her children and every child in her small town, to have access to a quality education in the arts. So she went to work and created from scratch a community arts program that has become nationally recognized and honored.

Jolene Edmunds Rockwood: *Building a Community
Arts Program*

I still remember my reluctance when my husband, Fred,
announced he had received a tempting job offer from a company in a town of about five thousand people in rural south-
eastern Indiana. A small midwestern town was never on my list
of places to live. I had just completed my graduate degree and
birthed my third child, and my oldest child was preschool age.
My husband assured me, "We'll only stay for a few years, get
as much experience as we can, and then we'll move on." After
a visit to the town and a strong sense that this was where we
were supposed to be, in 1977 we made the big move.

I immediately fell in love with the charm of a small community and the open acceptance of the town members, yet I found
myself longing for some of the opportunities I had had in a big
city. My friend Janel, who moved into town not long after we
did, noticed the same thing, so we started taking our kids into
Cincinnati (about an hour's drive each way) for music, drama,
and dance lessons. One day, as we were driving in the car, we
started dreaming about an arts program in our schools, so all
the students could benefit along with our own kids.

After attending an arts-in-education workshop in Indianap-
olis, Janel and I approached three public schools about starting a program. It was a hard sell at first. At the end of each
presentation, we passed around a sign-up sheet for any teachers who would be interested in having artists come into their
classrooms; six to eight takers at each school was enough to
get it rolling.

Next, we had to find grant money to fund the program. I
had never written a grant before, but I thought I could probably do it. Our first grant was $2,000 from the Indiana Arts

Commission, which covered half the cost of the program. To come up with the $2,000 cash match, Janel and I persuaded local businesses to donate $1,500 the first year. We solved the $500 deficit by inviting the owner of the biggest business in town to dinner, after which our children performed on the piano, violin, and cello. When we mentioned we were starting a program so all the children could have access to the arts, but were short on funds, he immediately wrote us a check for the remaining $500 and promised to support the program in the future. Over the next ten years, as demand grew, we increased the number and length of residencies; our expenditures went from $4,000 to $40,000 within ten years, and we consequently wrote larger and larger grants. Eventually, the National Endowment for the Arts in Washington, D.C., decided to use our program as an example of a successful arts-in-education program in their funding hearings before Congress.

To recognize our student artists, I started Young Artist Showcase, a program where students sign up to perform or have their work reviewed by professionals in the field, and then receive written feedback and ratings. We feature the winners in a community art show, recital, and published anthology. Showcase recognition has become prestigious and also looks very impressive on college applications.

Subsequently, I started a community arts council, so we could expand our arts programs beyond the schools to include the entire town, and soon the Rural Alliance for the Arts, or RAA, was born. The RAA started a community theater group, and in the past twenty years, we have produced more than forty musicals and plays, which involved thousands of local community members. The RAA also cosponsors the Batesville Music and Arts Festival, featuring a performance by the Cincinnati Symphony Pops. Currently, I am raising funds and community support to build a new performing arts center in our town.

Starting the arts-in-education program wasn't easy and it took a lot of hard work for many years—and tremendous support from my family—to establish and grow it. In fact, I'm still amazed at how the little idea that started in 1982 grew to be the thriving community arts program it is today.

BREAKING THINGS DOWN

When I arrived in New York I wanted to succeed so badly I had to square off with my perfectionism, muscling through the fear. I also learned a few tricks, such as breaking things down into small enough pieces that I wouldn't be overwhelmed, or telling myself to spend just five minutes putting everything together that I'd need, and then I could go do something else.

This is one of the reasons I eagerly participate in the twelve-week Resolutionary Challenge each January. Started by Heather Clayton Staker in 2008, the challenge focuses on process, breaking things down into baby steps so we can achieve set goals. Each day, ten points are possible, one point per task. The daily tasks typically include:

- Drink eight glasses of water
- Exercise thirty minutes
- Be ready to present myself to the world by 11:00 A.M.
- Eat two servings of fruit and three servings of vegetables
- Wash the dishes before going to bed
- Savor up to one small treat per day
- Set aside fifteen minutes just for me

In order to send perfectionism packing, the Resolutionary Challenge is organized so that even if I only do five of the ten assigned tasks per day, it's likely to be one or two more than I would have otherwise done. As a result, I get to feel good right away about my progress. If I don't have such a stellar showing on one day, I can reboot the next day. Furthermore, there are prizes like a gift certificate for a manicure for completing the challenge and for a score of 60 percent or better. We can each take a similar approach to the dreaming process, breaking our goal down into small, doable daily tasks. We can tailor our tasks to a specific dream (and award ourselves prizes). An example: "I will spend ten minutes a day working on a writing project." If I do, I get *(you name the prize)*.

When we're open to bootstrapping, almost by definition we've broken things down enough that we can cut through our need for flawlessness. When we do, we can accomplish more (because we procrastinate less) and model for our children how to cope with perfectionism. We can also stop doing something if we realize it's not worth finishing. We can try dreams out, knowing we don't have to marry every dream we date. Most importantly, we can happily and exuberantly take on the double-dog dare task of dreaming, without the paralyzing fear of failure.

TURNING OUR BACKS ON THE UNATTAINABLE

Bootstrapping also helps us recognize that there may be things we want to have, and learn whether or not they're actually attainable. If we start with what we have on hand, we'll move into the right dream for us. Here's a piece I've written about doing just that:

THE MIRROR OF ERISED

I'd been thinking all week about dreams that can't come true, coming to no conclusions, until I saw my daughter devour yet another Harry Potter book, and with Harry Potter on the brain, I went to bed. *Grapple with a problem. Grapple with it some more, and then go to sleep.* In others words, do as Psyche did, let the ants sort the seeds.

In the morning, the Mirror of Erised—a mirror that, as Harry Potter author J.K. Rowling describes, "shows us nothing more or less than the deepest, most desperate desire of our hearts"—came to mind.

When Professor Dumbledore discovers Harry secreted away in an unused chamber within Hogwarts Castle, entranced by the Mirror of Erised, he explains why the mirror is so beguiling and therefore dangerous: "You, who have never known your family, see them standing around you. Ronald Weasley, who has always been overshadowed by his brothers, sees himself standing alone, the best of all of them. However, this mirror will give us neither knowledge nor truth. Men have wasted away before it, entranced by what they have seen, or been driven mad, not knowing if what it shows is real or even possible.... It does not do to dwell on dreams and forget to live."

I suspect that most of us have a desperate desire of our heart, something we even desperately deserve, that we don't have and can't have—at least in the way we imagine.

Will you take a moment and think about what your desperate desire is, hold it in your hands, and examine it? Inside of this something we can't have, there are likely the seeds of a dream that is within reach.

Harry can't have his parents, but he can be surrounded by those he loves and who love him. Ron can't be an only child, but he can distinguish himself as he moves with Harry and Hermione through their hero's journey.

Haven't we all found ourselves enthralled by, or wasting away in front of, our own Mirror of Erised? I'm learning to walk away from the mirage and bootstrap my way into my life. No doubt you are too.

There's a great saying that is often heard in my circles: "Use it up, wear it out, make it do, or do without." We can dream big dreams, but those big dreams start with taking baby steps, breaking down dreams into very small pieces, beginning with the resources on hand. In other words, they start with bootstrapping. When we maximize what we have, avoiding the lottery approach to dreams, jettisoning our "perceived need" for outside resources, we can jumpstart the process of making our dreams a reality.

STARTING WITH WHAT WE HAVE...

A budget of money, time, or space shouldn't be about what we can't do or have, but how to make it happen.

        —Emily Orton, a marathoner and mother of five

- As you think about discovering your dream, what are two or three things you can do, starting with the time, money, space, and expertise you have right now?

When the tension is greatest and resources are most limited, people are actually a lot more open to rethinking the fundamental way they do business.

        —Clayton M. Christensen, author and professor

- What are your constraints as you move toward your dream? Is the dearth of resources an opportunity to rethink your plan, possibly improving your odds of success?

14

DATE YOUR DREAM

You've gone through the process of cataloguing your strengths, exploring the hopes you had when you were young, remembering what makes you feel strong, focused, fulfilled. As we look over our list of strengths, we begin to piece together potential dreams. Some months ago I discovered a website called SuperCook (supercook.com), a recipe search engine where you type in the ingredients you have on hand and it will find a recipe for you to make. I find this concept compelling, the premise being that we all have lots of "ingredients" on hand. In fact, I believe we have a lot more on hand, or a lot more possibilities available to us, than we realize.

When we bootstrap our way into a dream, we have a goal in sight and go in search of the necessary skills and resources to make it happen. In the SuperCook approach, we identify the skills, resources, and knowledge we already have on hand and see what we might make of them. That we have more available to us than we may think was illustrated nicely in a short-lived show on TLC titled *I've Got Nothing to Wear*. In this six-part series, a professional stylist assigns the guest's clothing to one of two categories: salvageable or unsalvageable. The unsalvagables are sent to the "chop shop," where three designers have been assigned to cull, rip, redesign, and re-sew the items into fresh, fashionable pieces (for example, an outdated pair of slacks might become an evening gown). In the meantime, the stylist shops with the guest for four or five classic items to complement the salvaged clothing. When the stylist creates a "look book" that shows the guest how to mix and match the salvaged clothes, the newly purchased classics, and the revamped pieces, the wardrobe makeover is complete.

As we figure out our dreams, I'd draw a number of comparisons: *Salvaged clothing or clothing that is wearable today* is a metaphor for our strengths, strengths we already possess, ingredients on hand, as it were. *Newly purchased classic items* are the one or two new skills we may need to achieve our dream; these skills are not necessarily expensive or even time-consuming to acquire. *Revamped or refashioned clothing:* just as each of us has clothes that we love, possibly inherited from our grandmothers or mothers, that no longer fit us or who we are, we also have strengths, qualities that may have even gotten us through tough times, that now must go to the chop shop for a repurpose (i.e. revamped or refashioned clothing). As we inventory our strengths, examine how we might repurpose longstanding skills, and acquire new ones, we are in effect figuring putting together a "look book" of our possibilities. Out of this book, we will find two or three dreams we'd like to try on for a day or two, dreams we'd like to explore.

Ingredients in search of a recipe, clothing in search of a personal style, strengths in search of a dream—possibilities really do abound. Once we have figuratively "typed in our ingredients" and the search engine of our imagination has generated a list of possible dreams that we can make happen, it's time to start writing them down.

You just be may be surprised by the consequence of doing so, as was Melissa Stanton, a former editor of *People* and *Life* magazines, and the author of *The Stay-at-Home Survival Guide: Field-Tested Strategies for Staying Smart, Sane, and Connected While Caring for Your Kids.*

Melissa Stanton: *Don't Just Think It, Ink It*

Was it my dream to be a stay-at-home mom?

No, at least I didn't think so. But I've recently realized that becoming a stay-at home mom, which I've been for nearly eight years, might have been an unintentional dream come true.

This past year, for the first time in my stay-at-home career, all three of my children were in full-day school. With my new-found freedom I started working through two decades–worth of files and boxes, including boxes from when I left my job at *People* magazine, where I was a senior editor. At the time, a confluence of events—my husband taking a job in Baltimore when his Wall Street–area employer hit hard times, my being a weekday single mother with a demanding career and long commute, September 11—led me to conclude that I needed to work a different way, and live a different way.

In the chaos surrounding my decision to leave a career I had aspired to and worked hard at for more than fifteen years, I didn't realize I was making one of my dreams come true. Nine months earlier I had participated in a career development workshop in which the instructor told us to write down three personal goals we wanted to achieve within a year. The activity's mantra:

"Don't just think it, ink it."

As I sorted through the old work papers, I found the class handout and my scribbled list of goals:

1. I will have a family-friendlier career.
2. I will have a second child.
3. My husband and I will be more financially secure and able to pay down some debt.

It turns out that within a year of "inking" those goals, I had achieved each one—although not in ways I ever imagined.

1. After leaving *People*, I started freelance writing from home.
2. Baby Number 2 materialized as Numbers 2 and 3.
3. My husband's new job enabled us to get by on one income.

My goals (or dreams?) had come true.

Navigating the huge transition from an active work life to a life dominated by domesticity led to another goal. I wanted to combine my "past life" as a writer and editor with my new life as a stay-at-home mom by writing a realistic, non-Mommy Wars "support-group-in-a-book" for, as one reviewer would so aptly describe, "any mom who has felt she has the best job in the world, and the worst job in the world, all within a two-minute time frame."

While some women love every minute of being a stay-at-home mom—and are, in fact, living their dream—many others struggle with the demands of being a 24-7 at-home mom. To them, stay-at-home motherhood isn't necessarily a calling. I believe stay-at-home parenting is a job, and stay-at-home moms are "working moms." No one loves her job every minute of the day. Not always loving stay-at-home motherhood doesn't mean a woman is a bad mother, or that she regrets leaving the workforce, or that she doesn't love her kids or appreciate her good fortune. It just means she needs a break, and she needs interests and activities independent of caring for kids.

After many, many rejections from agents and publishers who didn't want to do a "stay-at-home mommy book," or else wanted a book with a "strong" platform ("Mothers should stay home with their children" or "Mothers should stay in the workforce"), my pitch landed on the desk of an editor who had once been a stay-at-home mom. She understood the need for the book (which I researched and wrote at night while I cared for my kids by day) and championed it to publication.

Would the former me have ever dreamed that I'd someday write a book about stay-at-home motherhood? Absolutely not. But just as dreamers need to live in the real world, dreams—manifested as goals—emerge from our realities.

My new dreams, which I'll dare to "ink" here and not just think, are to:

1. Write a "support-group-in-a-book" for stay-at-home moms seeking to reenter the paid workforce.
2. Reenter the paid workforce myself, with a truly family-friendly career that allows me to earn decent money and do professional-level work without having to sacrifice my family to my job.

What dreams would you dare to ink and not just think?

Since inking this essay, Melissa has reentered the workforce with a "family-friendlier-than-before" career. While she still hopes to write a "support-group-in-a-book" for moms seeking paid employment, that goal is taking a bit longer to achieve due to her now-full plate, balancing work and family.

As you enumerated your strengths, you likely wrote down your thoughts and ideas, even scribbled in the margins here. I would encourage you to continue to do so. Ideas that intrigue you will also flit through your mind. If they persist, write them down. I imagine note cards tacked to a large corkboard, each card with a word or phrase describing a potential dream written on it. This is your pool of dreams. Maybe you already have a favorite, a dream that you know you want to pursue wholeheartedly. Or maybe, like me, you have a dozen half-formed dreams that you might want to try on. At this point, you must give yourself time to explore—to take a dream out for a test drive.

If you are a perfectionist like me, it is really, really hard to start. Which is why I believe in dating dreams—when we give ourselves permission to date dreams with a no-commitment clause, it's really quite liberating. That's precisely what Kristy Williams, a former Bain management consultant and corporate strategist who now focuses on motherhood, opted to do a few years ago.

Kristy Williams: *Five Dreams I Think I'll Date*

Goals have always been a central part of my life. I like feeling proactive and productive and enjoy the sense of accomplishment that comes once goals are achieved. As I read Whitney's article "Making Space for Your Dream," I realized that while I continue to set goals, I'm plumb out of dreams.

In the busy years after college, I worked challenging jobs, traveled to many places throughout the world, met a wonderful man whom I married, and became a mother. In the process, I achieved the dreams I set in high school and college. In all the excitement of those years, new dreams weren't really needed. The pace of my life has now slowed, making room for dreams once again.

But what do I dream of?

I want dreams I can work on now, recognizing that full realization may be fifteen to thirty years off, once the role of full-time mother lessens in intensity. Many weeks of introspection have yielded five dreams I'm going to consider. Each of the five potential dreams is something I enjoy, but until I spend some time with them, I won't know if they merit dream status. So, while I'm happily married, I'm going to spend some time dating this year—dating my dreams to determine which ones are right for me.

DREAM NO. 1: Writing (Of the Nonfiction Variety)

My first date has gone well—writing and publishing this post about my dreams has been engaging, stretching, and rewarding. I want to come up with two more topics and find two other places to publish. Future dates will involve considering how I can make writing a more consistent part of my life.

DREAM NO. 2: Business Consulting

I did this for a living and, on the whole, enjoyed it. I love reading about business and chatting with my husband about his start-up. My first few dates with this dream will be all brainstorming. How can I consult in my spare time? Who would be interested in short blocks of commitment? One option would be to focus on creatives: those selling their wares via a personal website or Etsy, or other small business owners. I could provide support in creating a strategy, identifying a focused market group, setting prices, etc.

DREAM NO. 3: Teaching

This can start simply, perhaps by inviting some friends for a one-off class/discussion. First date: come up with a topic I'm passionate about. Second date: develop the material and invite people to come. Further down the line this could lead to something more structured—maybe a class at the local high school (filled with underprivileged teens) on preparing for college.

DREAM NO. 4: Politics

My long-term dream may be to run for office. For now, my efforts will involve researching the candidates running for governor in California. If I like one of the candidates, I'll date some more by looking at ways to get involved in the campaign. Or I may keep this simple: get involved by joining the online dialogue on politically based sites.

DREAM NO. 5: Competitive Running/Triathlons

The competitive part is surely many, many years off, but in the meantime, I can get involved in racing. I'm going to identify five races that pique my interest and start by running in a local 10K.

With all the focus on dreams this year, I am bound to discover something that excites me and provides enlightenment, energy, and joyful anticipation as I work to determine who I want to become.

Kristy subsequently received two intriguing inquiries from small business owners in New York about short-term consulting gigs. Nothing ultimately came of these inquiries, but that's not important. The point of exploring is to explore. To *date dreams.* Or, as Madeleine Walburger wrote in chapter 5, to play with a concept and *dream dabble.*

A few years ago, I dated what felt like a rather frivolous dream. I'm not going to leave my husband and children and take up with a rock band, but when I saw a friend's blurb on the Ladies Rock Camp, a weekend fundraiser in which women learn how to play instruments and write songs, I knew this was something I didn't want to just imagine or think about; it was something I wanted to explore.

I noodled around with this possibility for several weeks. Earlier in the year, my husband, kids, and I had visited our friends Renee and Troy Tribe. Troy and the three oldest kids had started a rock band. After dinner, they performed '70s classics "Smoke on the Water" and "Takin' Care of Business" in their basement studio. It was a highlight of the vacation.

I found myself thinking, why not?

But I just imagined, and then my imagining was done, with no exploratory follow-up, which is what we often do. No surprise, really. We are primed to stop at imagining, whether it's because we don't want to be disappointed or vulnerable, or because we may not do whatever thing we want to explore very well. Or we don't want to be impractical. Why spend the time if we aren't really going to pursue something, to seriously commit to it?

There's an irony in this. If we will allow ourselves to move beyond imagining to exploring, knowing that we can say "no" at any point, it's really quite liberating. We have so many commitments, that we want and need to keep, to God, family, friends, community, work, and most importantly, to ourselves.

But there are some things we don't have to commit to. We get to do these things for a day, a week, even a month, and then if we want to, we can be done with it and go on to imagine and explore another possibility. Like Ladies Rock Camp.

As we begin to think about and explore our possibilities, it is quite likely that we will fall off the saddle. Trying on dreams for a few minutes or even a day will be uncomfortable for us because we are in essence asking for what we want. Because our family or friends—or even we—may label some dreams as "not sufficiently important," "frivolous," "fun," or "pointless," we may not end up following through. That is what happened with Ladies Rock Camp. I registered and made my hotel reservations for the camp months in advance, but two days before camp started, I cancelled my trip. I felt sad about it, but there are times when circumstances beyond our control prevent us from exploring. I wonder, though, if—more often than not—we simply lose our nerve. It's probably good for us to sort through the why of our decisions.

It's more important that we never, never, never give up exploring; when we fall off the saddle of our possibilities, we need to get right back up. Rebecca Ellsworth Menzie (beantown.menzie .org), a wife and mother who enjoys baking, quilting, gardening, triathlon-ing, and blogging, shares how her daughter taught her an important lesson about exploring possibilities and not giving up, even in the face of failure.

Rebecca Ellsworth Menzie: *Not a Track Star*

Sometime last fall, my fourteen-year-old, Christina, announced she wanted to do track. Imagine my surprise, considering I'd never seen Christina run, jog, or walk for exercise, not to mention that she hasn't participated in a team sport since elementary school soccer (I think she did two seasons). Honestly, I thought she was kidding, but she brought this up a couple more times, and then she went and signed herself up! The Saturday before track started, Christina suited up in workout clothes, borrowed my old running shoes, and said, "I'll be right back. I'm going to take a run." I scratched my head and chuckled. And she was off.

After a couple weeks, I asked Christina what event she was doing. She answered, "The 100. I can't run very far." Again, I was taken aback. I don't know any sprinters in our pedigree. Not one. "Any other events?" I ask. "Nope. Just the 100." After discussing her times, and how she fared in meets, it was clear that she was at the back of the pack for her single event. My husband and I wondered if the $240 athletic fee was worth it. But having that feeling that there was more to this for Christina than whether she was an emerging track star, we decided to support her. We made the extra trips to the school for practices and meets. We purchased workout clothes, the team sweat suit, and spiked shoes for our sprinter. We had conversations about the benefits of her participating in track.

We talked about how this is good for Christina's health. She's not growing in height anymore, and so it's important to be active in order to stay in good shape. She can always go jogging—it requires minimal gear, just get up and go. Jogging gives quick positive boosts to mental and physical well-being. It's good for your bones.

While we asked about her times and placement at meets, that has always been secondary to how much effort she puts into her races. We asked questions like: How do you feel about how things went? What went well? Is there anything you'd like to change? Christina has come in last place *often*. At first, this was embarrassing and discouraging for her. No one likes coming in last place. *But since when is last place equivalent to failure?* I shared with her how I quit the track team in high school because I was too scared to compete. I was afraid of not doing well. I let my fear of failure keep me from what could have been a great experience on the track team. To see my daughter get out there and go for it regardless of where she places, and having the confidence to sign up for a sport she knew nothing about before high school, makes me beyond proud...

So, no, Christina's not a track star, but she's a star nonetheless.

Rebecca clearly admires her daughter's refusal to back down from her dream of running track, even when she has come in last place many times. Sometimes our children can be our greatest examples, and in this case, Christina is teaching her mother how to try on a dream.

Part of dating dreams is that, just like first dates, we can sometimes be quite uncomfortable and things can go badly when we explore; we are in uncharted terrain. *Here's a post I wrote on my blog after a particularly tough week.*

WORTH DOING BADLY

Always be a beginner at something.
—Bill Buxton, senior researcher at Microsoft

We need to get over what we were taught in school. Look at Google. Everything is always in beta.
—Paul Gillin, technology journalist

If a thing is worth doing, it is worth doing badly.
—G.K. Chesterton, nineteenth-century
philosopher and writer

When I read the above quotes, I feel myself physically relax, perfectionism fading away. Because the fact is, anything really worth doing, from parenting to marriage to career to friendship to dreams, we sometimes do rather badly.

This last week I did things so badly I just wanted to quit. Which is why having my friend Lisa Boyce quote G.K. Chesterton was a gift. If we're doing things badly, maybe it means that we're doing things worth doing, that we're fully engaged in our lives, our relationships, and our dreams.

Be a beginner.

Be in beta.

Do things badly.

As you discover your dreams and begin to dabble, you may feel some amalgam of thrill and fear, and maybe even become defensive. That is when you know you are getting close, as happened with Janna Taylor, the founder of Mind Full Tutors (mind fulltutors.com), located on the Upper East Side of Manhattan.

Janna Taylor: *If You Get Defensive, You're Getting Close*

In fall 2007, I opened Mind Full Tutors, a tutoring company located on the Upper East Side of Manhattan. Even though starting a tutoring business had been my dream for several years, I resisted pursuing it like a stubborn mule.

Prior to receiving a Master's of Education at Harvard, I'd helped build a successful tutoring company. But when I graduated, I took a job working for a nonprofit teacher education program with no plan to start a tutoring business. Even though my work for the nonprofit was meaningful, I was unhappy. The job responsibilities did not play to my strengths and were far from the "action" of educating students.

When I complained to friends about my job, many responded with, "When are you going to start your tutoring company?" Each time, I met this encouragement with defensive responses such as, "There is no way I can do that," "I can't even think about that right now," or "Maybe someday...I don't know."

I have wondered—why was I defensive?

First, I was protecting my heart. I fervently wanted this dream to be a reality. But to pursue the dream would be to expose it to possible failure. I wondered if my heart could bear the disappointment.

Secondly, I was deflecting guilt for not acting authentically. I knew in my bones that part of living authentically was to start my own tutoring company. Because I knew it was going to be difficult and risky, I resisted.

These two factors blinded me to the possibility of success.

After several more months of job dissatisfaction, I decided to take a chance on what my friends and family could see, and what I had lost sight of. I wrote a business plan and five months later opened Mind Full Tutors. When I shared this news with my loved ones, all of the responses were akin to, "Finally!"

So what were my friends seeing that I wasn't?

My friends saw an open road to success, where I saw barricades and roadblocks. They saw abilities, where I saw deficiencies. They saw, "Why not?" and I saw, "Because..." They saw my need to live with passion and purpose, and I saw a need to compromise because of fear.

I've learned that others can play an important role in anchoring us to our dreams. They remind us of what we can and are meant to accomplish in this life. While it is true that some people can distract us from our dreams, those who know us best often see us for what we are—women of great ability and purpose.

Mind Full Tutors has been in business for almost a year now. My heart feels alive and I know that I am making difference in the world every day—one student at a time.

It is often true that when we are close to diving into a dream and we somehow sense that the advice we are receiving from those we love is right, it terrifies us, and so we reject it. I remember that being true four years ago with Rose Park Advisors. When

I first started speaking with the Christensens about launching a hedge fund, I thought, "I'll just work on this for awhile, it will be temporary." When my husband would say, "Why don't you do this?" I'd think, "Oh no, I couldn't possibly."

A dream I dated this past year was designing a dress for the Shabby Apple dress design contest. Because I don't draw, I wasn't going to enter, but I loved to sew as a young girl. I have an acquired competency of pulling together people and ideas (in this case I asked a talented artist to help me). Most importantly, I wanted to do this "just because," and it was important for me to be respectful of my wishes. So I dabbled.

I'm also exploring more intently my desire to produce a documentary. I know it will involve women—and probably dreams of some kind. Beyond that, I don't know. My innate talent around music should serve me well.

My acquired competencies of building and running a business will also come in handy, as will having learned to craft a narrative. Before really pursuing this, there's a lot more dating I'd need to do, given that a real script and financing would be required, but it's a dream that I want to explore. Who knows—maybe my dream that Rose Park Advisors' portfolio will eventually include capital devoted to women-owned businesses will lead to a documentary? I don't know yet. And I don't need to. Right now I'm exploring, dabbling, dating. It's in my look book of possibilities.

DABBLING, DATING, DELINEATING...

I believe God made me for a purpose, but he also made me fast. And when I run I feel His pleasure.

—Eric Liddell, in the Academy
Award–winning film *Chariots of Fire*

- Over the past few chapters, you've likely had many ideas about your strengths come to mind. If you haven't already, will you write them down, perhaps on an index card and lay them out in front of you, creating a look book of your possibilities?

If a thing is worth doing, it is worth doing badly.
—G.K. Chesterton, nineteenth-century
philosopher and writer

- What two or three dreams are you ready to explore? Will you not just think it, but ink it? If no, why?
- At the beginning of a new year, have you ever written down what you wanted to accomplish (without making resolutions, just a "nice-to-do" list), and gone back a year or two later only to recognize that the mere act of "inking it" moved you toward a dream?
- About what possibilities have you been imagining or daydreaming, but not yet explored?
- What do you want to do enough that you are willing to do it badly? This can be an important barometer of whether we want to move from exploring or dabbling to doing a dream.
- Is there something that you've gotten defensive about, only to realize that it's because you were getting close to *your* dream?

15

DOUBLE-DOG DARE!

Whether we've decided exactly what our dream is or we continue to experiment with two or three possibilities, there are times when we need to simply "double-dog dare" to dream. Contemplating a dream is one thing, actually "doing" a dream is another, and the reality of pursuing a dream may require courage, boldness, and daring.

In the parenting book *Mind in the Making: The Seven Essential Life Skills Every Child Needs,* Ellen Galinsky, a child education expert and cofounder of the Families and Work Institute, writes that one of the essential skills we need to teach our children is how to take on challenges. Galinsky explores this topic not by tackling perfectionism, but by examining how children learn to manage stress. Citing research done by Megan Gunnar, a professor at the University of Minnesota and an expert on stress and coping in children, Galinsky writes, "If you never allow your children to exceed what they can do, how are they going to manage adult life—where a lot of it is managing more than you thought you could manage?" She explains that one of the best ways for children to learn how to manage stress is by watching their parents model how they manage theirs.

By taking on our challenges, we teach our children to take on theirs, and give them the ability to dream. Further, it's only when we move beyond what we know we can do and take a risk—or double-dog dare—that we can make our dreams happen.

DARING TO BE A STAY-AT-HOME MOM

The tone of this book notwithstanding, one of the biggest dares a woman can take is to become a stay-at-home mom. It's a dare that requires a thousand *nos* to naysayers in order to say *yes* to her dream. And I don't mean the dream of bearing children, but of pouring energy into the rearing of children, opting out of the workforce to do so, and then claiming their power as mothers. Rachael Hutchins is a prime example of this kind of daring.

Rachael Hutchins: *When I Grow Up*

I had a tumultuous upbringing, and I remember thinking that when I grew up and had my own family, it wouldn't be like that, that I would provide my children with stability. I felt compelled to correct the mistakes my parents had made by becoming the best mother I could possibly be. To do this, I felt I needed to be an at-home mother. Making this decision early in life was detrimental to my college studies because I really didn't have any academic goals. All I wished and dreamed and hoped for was to become a mother. The pull of that dream was so strong I couldn't envision any other options for my life.

During my first year of college, I met and became engaged to a great young man. Despite my parents' concerns (and mine), even though I was only eighteen, I moved forward with confidence, given my conviction that marriage and motherhood were the right, in fact the only, paths for me. Nine months later, we joyfully welcomed our first child. I felt peace upon her arrival, that we had made the right decision in having children immediately, and that I was doing exactly what I wanted and needed to be doing. Mothering was a role I arrived at very naturally. It did not feel like a sacrifice.

After we welcomed two more perfect little girls to our family and dealt with my postpartum depression, we made the decision to stop having children. I was only twenty-five. I felt like a failure, as I had envisioned having a large family. For a while it felt as if my dream had died. But, just as having children was a right decision, stopping at three was also right.

Motherhood is a wonderful, exhausting, sometimes overwhelming, and often thankless job. I feel most discouraged when I believe I've failed my children by being short-tempered or emotionally distant, or when I see my negative behaviors in them. It's discouraging when we can't afford to provide them with more opportunities. I also feel down when I encounter mothers who seem to be doing their job—my job—so much better than I do. That's really hard. And yet, as I've I known from the moment our first daughter arrived, I have given my children 100 percent, and I know I'm giving my children a better upbringing than the one I received. I take consolation in that.

My oldest daughter recently called home from school to say she had forgotten her gym shoes (not an infrequent occurrence) and she asked me to bring them in for her. I did, and later that day she said, "Mom, I'm so glad you're home so you can bring me something if I forget it." When one of the girls was sick and stayed home from school, she'd say, "Mom, I'm so glad you stay at home so you can take care of me when I'm sick. What would I do if you were at work?" It has meant a lot to me to be able to do these small things for my children because, in doing so, I see myself becoming the kind of mother I want to be.

My accomplishments may seem small to many, but to me they are huge. In devoting my life to my children, I have truly found myself. I have experienced exponential growth in my thirteen years of mothering and, thanks to the influence my children have had on me, have come so very far from the nineteen-year-old young woman I was when I gave birth to my first child. Now that my children are in school full-time, I am, at the age of thirty-two, excited about what else may lie ahead. But regardless of what I go on to achieve in my life, nothing will be as important to me, or as fulfilling, as being a mother.

After a childhood rife with instability, Rachael Hutchins has truly taken on mothering. She has made a conscious decision, declared her dream, and is daring to give her mind and heart to her mothering. It's not always in the perfect way she had imagined, and there are likely moments of trepidation as she wonders if she can pull off what she hadn't seen done, but she is doing it.

DREAMING AMIDST UNCERTAINTY

As we grow older, it may take a double-dog dare to continue pursuing our dreams in the face of circumstances we cannot control—like aging. That has been true for Lisa Poulson, a public relations executive who is single, just learning to knit, and lives in a lovely apartment with four walk-in closets in San Francisco.

Lisa Poulson: *Dreaming 5.0*

The great Roman philosopher Epictetus said, "Happiness and freedom begin with a clear understanding of one principle: some things are within our control, some things are not."

Oh, how I wish I could attain this happiness and freedom. Instead, I rage and I pine.

Against the aging process.

To wit, my arms have become the consistency of melting ice cream, as if they were slipping from custard to liquid inside of a bag. When I bend over, my belly looks like lumpy pudding saturating a hammock.

My eyes are circled in lines. My knees shriek when I stand up after watching a movie—I limp down the stairs holding the rail, amazed and yet unsurprised at the betrayal.

Also, I can't see. I can't see who's on the phone without my glasses. I can't read the newspaper. I can't read a prescription bottle.

And I am only forty-seven.

People tell me I look great for my age (whatever that means). I exercise (cardio and Pilates), try to eat the right foods, etc. I do try to control what's happening to my body. But somewhere inside I know it is largely futile. I know I have turned the irrevocable corner from growth to decay, and I know that this is beyond my control.

Perhaps it is because I am female, and therefore trained to be deeply invested in my appearance, or perhaps it is because I am vain, and am therefore deeply invested in my appearance, but these changes pierce every part of me. Bette Davis was right—old age is no place for sissies.

It is not just my face and ligaments that are aging, but my soul, my mind, my perception of the future, my priorities, my regrets, my fears, my hopes. How does one navigate the path ahead after turning that irrevocable corner?

Epictetus also said, "Circumstances do not rise to meet our expectations. Events happen as they do. People behave as they are. Embrace what you actually get."

In the second half of life one needs new methods, new rules. One sets aside broad hopes and dreams for a glorious future full of adventures. One sets aside hopes for springy knees and smooth skin. One learns that the most graceful thing to do is to embrace what you actually get, what you actually have.

I'll be fifty in three years. My plan is to work on embracing what I actually have, building depth about what I already know and who I already am and who I already love. This is my process for devising Life 5.0—my life at fifty—the new version of myself.

It's a quieter way to dream, and a narrower way to dream, but nonetheless a deep way to live a life.

FACING OUR FEARS

Dreaming requires courage. Taking on our dreams is a bit like walking into a tunnel. As we contemplate the entrance to a dream, it may be unnerving, but while we are still surrounded by the known, there is a surge of armchair-dreaming adrenaline. Once inside the tunnel, we can be shrouded by second-guessing and self-doubt: "What was I thinking when I decided to do X, Y, or Z?" goes the refrain.

Then what? Some days we'll consider retreat. Two years into my different dream, a headhunter called me about returning to sell-side research. I took more than twenty-four hours to say no, even though I knew I would say no, just because it felt good to be wanted. Other days we'll advance, full of derring-do, willing to do whatever is required. (For example, to finance our dream, my husband and I decided to sell our home, which was a bold and somewhat scary decision at the time.) When any of us faces our fears and conquers the unknown, we trust that we'll again move into the known, confident that it will be a better known because we'll be more of who we are.

Tensie (pronounced TAWN-see) Whelan, president of the Rainforest Alliance (rainforest-alliance.org), didn't walk. She ran through her fear, taking on the challenge of her husband's sudden death while she was pregnant with their first child. She has translated her tragedy into daring to make her late husband's dream come true.

Tensie Whelan: *Seeing the Rainforest and the Trees*

I am not so sure when the dream started. Perhaps it was as a young teenager on a canoe trip with my family in the Quebec wilderness listening to loons and wolves sing a duo across the lake. Or perhaps it started when I was a ten-year-old visiting my grandparents in Mexico and seeing poverty like I had never seen before. Or perhaps it was just being the bossy older sister who needed to find something meaningful to do after her younger siblings grew up.

But my dream has always been to make a difference—in a big way. In what way wasn't clear at the beginning, but I knew I wanted to work in another country. I wanted to learn about other ways of doing things. Learn what mattered. Learn why people do what they do. Most of all, I wanted to learn what my place in it all would be.

I always cared about environmental issues. My first job after graduate school was working for World Wildlife Fund in Washington, D.C., and then as an environmental journalist in

Sweden and Central America. But it was not until my husband, Johan Ashuvud, an environmental economist, died in a car crash at age twenty-seven that I decided I was going to pursue efforts to make a difference for the planet *in a big way*. My husband could no longer pursue his dreams. I decided I would pursue our dreams for him.

Funny thing about surviving a tragedy like having your husband die after six months of marriage *and* being three months pregnant: you realize you can do anything. Really. Anything.

So I went after the dream. His dream. Our dream. My dream. I—we—wanted to radically transform how we all interact with the environment in order to create a better world for our children and their children, but also for all the beautiful plants and animals that share this amazing place with us.

Today, I'm the president of the Rainforest Alliance, an international organization that works in seventy countries to transform how we interact with nature and one other. (I'm also the mother of a lovely twenty-one-year-old daughter who looks a lot like her father.) We work with millions of small producers of crops, CEOs of big companies, and consumers to transform standard business practices. The candy manufacturer Mars is one example: in working with the farmers, foresters, and hotel managers to adapt their environmental, social, and economic practices to comply with our sustainable management standard, we help to ensure all their cocoa is sustainable. Chiquita has had all of its bananas certified by us. As a result, the farms these companies buy from have protected wildlife and their habitat, reforested native trees, reduced chemical use, improved worker housing and working conditions—and they've increased their yields in the process.

That's the other part of the dream, to improve conditions for people as well as the planet; I've never believed you could separate the two. When I visit a Rainforest Alliance–certified operation, the people working there are incredibly proud of all they've accomplished. Their farms or forests or hotels look very different than the norm, and people around them begin to copy them. On one of my visits to Colombia a group of macho coffee farmers with machetes began to compete with each other over how many migratory bird species they had identified on their respective farms. Such a conversation would *not* have happened before the Rainforest Alliance came into their lives.

So the dream is one that many others are now dreaming with me. Together we are translating our dreams into reality. It's exhausting. But it feels really, really good.

DARING TO DECIDE

Author and entrepreneur Seth Godin writes: "We hate to decide. We avoid deciding. We hide from it.... Once someone decides, they almost always succeed...." Whatever our dream, it's important to make a choice, to take things on, and then own what we choose. But that's hard to do, which is why descending into the underworld was Psyche's fourth task and not her first. Without the practice of establishing priorities, gathering needed resources, and learning to delegate and achieve goals, she would likely have failed at her fourth task, the critical undertaking of which was daring to say *no* to three people who would ask for her help in order to instead say *yes* to her beloved.

One of the ways we can decide to say yes to our beloved is to actually learn from one another how to dream. Heather Clayton Staker (see chapter 13), for example, a cofounder and former CFO of Karaiega LLC, now Yoostar Entertainment, and mother of four, has gained valuable momentum for her own dreams as she and her husband have worked in tandem to support and facilitate each other's dreaming.

Heather Clayton Staker: *Practical Tips When You Sleep with a Dreamer*

Eight years ago I married a dreamer. Not just your average big idea guy: my man has developed three patents, launched two companies, written treatments for eight screenplays, and relied on spreadsheets to track his personal projects. His favorite date night is to recline on our carport high atop a Hawaiian mountainside and watch the trade winds push the clouds briskly across the starry canopy—while we brainstorm new products and business models.

On the bright side, my life with Allan Staker will never be boring. But living with an inventor has its complexities. So the second you find your significant other dabbling in the elusive, heed these tips, girlfriend:

Live free or die: Face it. Your family's cash flow is not going to be the same as it would be if you had married a doctor. Expect to get payoffs in bright bursts, and then wait indefinitely for your next hit. Our best financial decision was to become apartment managers, which afforded us free rent during the riskiest part of our last venture. Go to your county's tax assessor office and request a tax roll, which is a list of properties in your area, their owners, and addresses. We used this list to contact several apartment owners until we convinced one of them to hire us as his on-site managers.

Slash your costs: Next time Allan feels the urge to innovate, he will have to order the moving PODS (Portable On Demand Storage) first. Why? Because groceries in, say, Texas, are 46 percent cheaper on average than in Honolulu where we live, and housing is 62 percent cheaper. In Fred Brock's *Live Well on Less Than You Think*, the author's first rule is to flee from high cost-of-living areas. To see how far your savings will go in another city, check out a cost-of-living calculator. We will not attempt another start-up before moving to a lower-cost launching ground.

Stoke your sense of humor: During our last rollercoaster start-up, we had to fight to keep the tone of our marriage from mirroring the ride of the project. Humor was the key that saved our marriage from tanking when the business took a dive. Our favorite funny shows include *Envy,* in which Jack Black plays an inventor who strikes it ultra rich; *Duplex,* which is only funny if you're apartment managers; and several *Saturday Night Live* shorts, like the classic Garth and Kat dress rehearsal version. And please, *no* talking about business or inventions after lights out.

Look to the rainbow: I imagine Allan will never have a traditional career path. Thus we have moved seven times and lived in three states during our eight years of marriage. Our current home in Honolulu is certainly lush and beautiful, but our kids often ask when we will move back to "America." One night, when I was feeling homesick, Allan and I decided that, to buoy us up, we would to try to visit every waterfall we could find on the Hawaiian Islands. Recently, we flew our four small children on a twenty-four-hour trip to the Big Island to visit Umauma Falls. This new quest brought me tremendous joy.

Eliminate avoidable risk: Next time we undertake a new venture, Allan and I will be smarter about our business model and financing plan first. With our last venture, we could have eliminated some of the financial headaches and product viability risks if we had played the game differently. As Clark Gilbert and Matthew Eyring point out in the *Harvard Business Review* article "Beating the Odds When You Launch a New Venture," entrepreneurs can prevent future pain by avoiding important uncertainties before going further with a project. This includes prototyping quickly and doing quick-hit market research to make sure that the fundamental idea is sound, before pouring in cash.

See afar off: In the book of Moses, God tells Enoch he is angry with his people, for "their hearts have waxed hard, and their ears are dull of hearing, and their eyes cannot see afar off." Perhaps the greatest pitfall to avoid as the lover of an inventor is myopia—the inability to see "afar off." For all my stressing about my worn-out Isaac Mizrahi clothes from Target, I am married to a one-of-a-kind man with an unusual gift. When we were dating, Allan warned me that his theme song was Bon Jovi's "Livin' on a Prayer." Decades from now, I believe we will both look back on our start-up early marriage days as a time when he beckoned me, as that song states, to *"take my hand and we'll make it I swear,"* and we did.

Heather is pursuing her dream of being a mother as well as partnering with her husband in the pursuit of his dreams. They are courageously pursuing a career path outside the norm, which takes daring and a commitment to support one another, through bad times and good. Their marriage is stronger because they dream big and dream together. As they dream together, Heather and Allan are teaching their children to dream.

Sometimes taking things on means that we just suit up and show up, and that we get into the game of our life with an attitude of "I will not be defeated." Which is what Jenny Clawson did.

Jenny Clawson, is a five-time entrepreneur, whose launched company Mobonics (mobonics.com) won at TwilioCon2011, and received funding from TwilioFund and from VC investor Dave McClure's 500 Startups. Jenny has experienced her own road of trials on her way to a dream, using pure determination to muscle through fear.

Jenny Clawson: *Resistance*

Resistance. We have all felt it at some point or another. We set a goal, have every intention of keeping that goal and realizing that dream, and then comes the morning. The morning where we wake up and think, what was I thinking? Did I really say I would do that? Yep, that's resistance. And resistance is not a morning person.

Last year was my year of resistance. To everything, really. I graduated from B-school with the idea that I would take a break from achievement for a while. I wanted a break from the endless nights of Excel spreadsheets and PowerPoint presentations. I felt I deserved it. Before going back to school I had launched a business, so I had spent the past four years working around the clock. And I was exhausted. I dreamed of landing some cushy job with a paycheck, so I could then work on more important things, like getting a tan and perfecting my golf swing.

You can imagine how well that turned out. The cushy job did not materialize, and I was stuck. Trapped, really. In the belly of the whale. But unlike Jonah, I wasn't swallowed up for three days; it was for an entire year. No matter how hard I tried, I couldn't seem to get "the job." The more I interviewed, the more confused I became as to what I even wanted. What really started to worry me was not that I couldn't get hired, but that I didn't really want to get hired. After praying, pondering, exploring, I realized that I didn't want a "job," I was looking for a purpose. I wanted to know what God wanted me to do with my life. I begged, pleaded, bargained. And the answer came. It crept into my mind, whispering the one thing I didn't want to hear. And then it became louder, nagging me incessantly, saying "it's time to launch a business."

So I did what any Jonah would do. I ran in the opposite direction. I watched a lot of Food Network channel. I went to the gym. I worked a little, and I cried a lot. I resisted and resisted until I went through all five phases of the grieving process: (1) Denial and Isolation, (2) Anger, (3) Bargaining, (4) Depression, and (5) Acceptance. It was at step four that I knew I was in trouble. Not achieving was not working for me, yet I just couldn't do it. Every time I sat down to work on this new business, I became completely overwhelmed. The thought of it exhausted me in body, mind, and spirit. Hello, resistance.

Because I was incapable at the time of working toward my dream and had a lot of extra time on my hands, I channeled my energy into Tony Horton's P90x exercise program. This program is known around the world for being an absolutely grueling, intense workout, geared to cause muscle confusion. So you are literally sore for thirteen weeks. And the workouts are long, an hour and fifteen minutes to an hour and a half each day, six days a week.

Nine weeks into the program, resistance reared its ugly head again. It was 10:30 P.M., and I still had the yoga workout to do. I despised that workout. It was ninety minutes long—which is an eternity in downward dog. I sat on the couch rationalizing to myself, "it's O.K. to take a day off. You can just do two routines the next day. No one will know." In the midst of this inner battle, I remembered something Horton said on his DVD (paraphrasing): Some days you will not be able to do as much as other days, but just keep putting the DVD in and pushing play.

So I said aloud, "Jenny, just get up and push play."

And that's when I faced resistance head on and beat it. That's when I learned that it is in the I-don't-feel-like-it-but-I-am-going-to-do-it-anyway times that we make the real progress.

To live our dreams, we don't need grand visions. We just need to show up. Every day, even when we don't feel like it, even when something "urgent" comes up. Even when we are scared out of our minds and completely overwhelmed. We show up.

So I have launched out—out of the whale's belly and into the tumultuous sea. But I am out. And I am showing up.

'

Many of us arrive at a point of paralysis when it comes to diving into our dream. As Jenny learned, sometimes the only way through is to simply show up and do what needs to be done.

Whether our dream is to parent, paint, write a book, produce a film, or start a business, sometimes we'll achieve what we set out to do, sometimes we won't. Almost always what we *do* achieve will be different than what we originally envisioned. But, ultimately, it's the aspiring, not the actual achieving, that most matters. In her book *Simple Abundance*, Sarah Ban Breathnach makes this distinction: "Expectations are the emotional investment that our ego makes in a particular outcome. When we use expectations to measure a dream's success, we tie stones around our soul. Dreams [may] call for a leap of faith, a trusting that [Providence] will be our net, but they set our soul soaring."

Though achieving our dreams is ultimately somewhat out of our control, who we become in the striving isn't. Winston Churchill's admonition, "Never, never, never, never give up" has always resonated with me. Thus our family's derivative saying, "Johnsons never give up!" Even if you don't know what your dream is exactly, *never, never, never, never* give up dreaming.

Making a dream happen involves risk: risk of failure, risk associated with change. Taking on that risk requires facing our fears and courageously moving ahead with determination. Part of saying yes to ourselves is learning to say no to detractors. Part of saying yes is simply saying yes, I will dare to dream.

DERRING-DO...

If you never allow your children to exceed what they can do, how are they going to manage adult life—where a lot of it is managing more than you thought you could manage?
—Ellen Galinsky, author and cofounder of the
Families and Work Institute

- As you dream, what have you managed that you thought you couldn't? Are you giving your children that opportunity?

Never, never, never, never give up.
—Winston Churchill, former British prime minister

- Once you decide on a dream you want to make happen, do you ever find that you have to suit up and show up, repeatedly, until the dream happens?

Wherever you see a successful business, someone once made a courageous decision.
—Peter Drucker, writer and management consultant

- Is there a courageous decision you need to make?
- What circumstances beyond your control have you faced, even as you continued to dream?
- Is there anything that you very much want, but the unknown is so unnerving you are considering giving up?
- Why do we need to learn to say no before we can really say yes to our dreams?

Epilogue
Dreaming Again and Again

In writing this book, I dared to dream. Through this nine-month process of organizing my ideas, writing because I have something to say, bringing together a Dare to Dream team of women who likewise have something to say, I'm finding my voice and I'm becoming the hero of my story.

As I complete this manuscript, I'm being invited to dream again. Two days ago, Dana King (see chapter 13) shared a link with me to an open casting call for a Mark Burnett–produced reality TV show in which the prize is your own talk show.

Dana's words to me: "*I dare you.*"

My thoughts: I want to go to this audition. I'm scared. I shouldn't do it. It's impractical. I'll have to fill out a lengthy application, stay a day over in New York, and wake up well before dawn. I'll likely get my feelings hurt. For a *long shot!* But, when I shared this idea with my childhood friend Liz Economy, she declared, "What have you got to lose?" Liz was polite enough not to have said, "Walk your talk."

And she's right. So I've decided, yes, I'm going to suit up, and show up at the casting call. Will my application even get reviewed? They only look at the first five hundred. If my application does get a viewing, will they like me? Will I make the first cut? I don't know. All are outcomes I can't control. If I don't get to audition, maybe I'll make a video. If I do, but I get cut, I'll be sad. My feelings may even be hurt. But I'll recover, and I'll know that I took on my dream to create a platform from which I can invest not only in stocks, but also in people, concepts, and dreams. And because dreaming is a process, when I dream—when you dream—we are invited to dream again.

DREAMING IN STAGES

How this process unfolds is different for each one of us. For some, our dreams center on the professional track. For many women in early adulthood, the dream of being an at-home mother takes priority, while other dreams are deferred or done part-time. As we discover our way to making our dreams happen, when we trust ourselves, our intuition, we'll know which dream to pursue, as well as when and how. That has been the case with Margaret Woolley Busse, a Harvard-trained MBA who someday hopes to run for political office, but has taken a leave from full-time employment in order to be at home with her young children.

Margaret Woolley Busse: *100% Wool*

"And you'll have root beer in your drinking fountains!"
Dreams start in funny ways. I was in the second grade listening to the speeches of would-be student body presidents, each one wanting our vote. (Although as a lowly second-grader, I couldn't vote!) And here was this guy, promising that if elected,

he would apparently defy the principal, parents, and probably the plumbing by getting our favorite soft drink to stream out of fountains.

I didn't buy it. I understood at that moment how the game of politics works. Get votes by offering potentially impossible but tantalizing promises. I suppose it was a loss of innocence, of sorts. To my relief as a disenfranchised second-grader, the root beer–pusher didn't win.

Skeptical as I was, I was also enamored by the idea of democracy—that people can affect government by electing leaders who reflect their values and beliefs, and can even become those elected leaders. In high school I ran for senior class president. Given that my last name was "Woolley," I used "Don't Vote for a Polyester Politician, Vote 100% Wool" as a campaign slogan. Corny, I know, but the theme resonated with me. I didn't want to be a root beer–pusher.

But the trouble remains. Whether it's candidates for grammar school president or for the U.S. Senate, the formula for winning is usually the same: promulgate clever, yet often meaningless, campaign slogans and offer slick speeches with sticky-sweet, root beer–drinking-fountain promises. Of course, when elected officials don't deliver on those promises, we become cynical, and cynicism can lead to something even worse: apathy.

I didn't become apathetic. I was passionate about the idea of policymaking. I loved economics and found political philosophy fascinating. But I did become cynical about elected officials, so I aspired instead to be a high-level appointed official—secretary of state, perhaps? Yet, as I progressed through college and professional workdom, it became more apparent to me that without having a long, concentrated, full-time career (not to mention high-level connections, brains, and luck), becoming secretary of state might be a little unrealistic. I knew I wanted to marry, have children, and take care of them.

I also observed that elected officials had more varied back-
grounds than your average cabinet member. And I am nothing
if not pragmatic.

Still, I didn't know if I could stomach going the elected
route—the campaigning, the negotiating, the wheeling and
dealing. I didn't want to be "polyester." Yet a few experiences
in college helped me clarify my own strengths: I managed a
campaign for a friend running for student body president and
discovered that not only was I good at campaigning, I loved it.
Later, I found my time in a mock legislative assembly exhilarat-
ing as I negotiated with others and won support for the "bill"
I was advocating. After experience, reflection, and plain old
time, my dream re-crystallized: elected office.

Fast forward through a few academic degrees, real-world
employment, and marriage, and here I am, living in Suburbia,
USA, with four tiny kids that I care for on a full-time basis. The
choices that led me here have been very deliberate, and made
without regret. I'm looking forward to the day when I can run
for public office, but during this intense period of motherhood,
the time is not right. And I'm not prepared. Still, between all
the diaper changes, meal-making, and exuberance of little children (my joy!), I'm preparing. I've pounded the pavement for
issues I really care about—with children in tow. I started a blog
where I can articulate (to myself, if no one else) my thoughts
about policy and politics. I write letters to the editor of my local
newspaper. I read. I vote. I listen to my neighbors. I serve on
my town's planning board. These activities are not just means
to an end, however. At the root of my desire to serve in public
office is my deep interest in understanding and improving government, along with my personal delight in building community and interacting with people and hearing their ideas.

And yet, with all this desiring and doing, I'm surprised by
how much I fear my dream. I strive to be that "100% Wool"

person of my high school ideals, but I see the pressure on elected officials to compromise their integrity, offering up the adult equivalent of sticky-sweet root beer. I also know that fulfilling this dream means making it a reality, and reality rarely reflects our glossy conjurations. Still, when the time is right, I will dare to do it. And that's its own variety of 100% Wool.

It isn't simple. Life isn't a breeze as we dream. As Margaret Woolley Busse wrote, "reality rarely reflects our glossy conjurations." But there is happiness, hope smiling before us, as we claim a central place in their lives or, as Julie Berry (julieberrybooks .com), the author of the young adult novels *The Amaranth Enchantment* and *Secondhand Charm*, describes, as we "embrace round."

Julie Berry: *Embracing Round*

In fiction, we're fascinated by characters who, like real people, are flawed, unpredictable, conflicted, self-deceived, smart yet irrational, courageous yet fragile, prudent yet occasionally reckless, irresponsible yet sometimes noble, righteous yet privately naughty. Books I love best confront and embrace their characters' roundness. The author's empathy for, amusement at, and delight in the little cast of loonies shines through on every page.

When my friend Kimberly Carlile posed the question, "Are we flat characters or round?" During a salon-style discussion about the transformative power of literature, I realized something about myself that I hadn't articulated until I put it in the language of literary character.

I occupy many roles—wife, mother, author, marketing director, choir director, neighbor, friend, daughter, citizen, and so on. But what character do I play as I occupy these roles? Is it an honest one?

In my town I often portray The Frazzled Mother of Four Rambunctious Boys. This is scarcely an artistic stretch. I've spent years polishing my performance. The community is happy to place me there. I get a lot of, "Four? All yours? God bless you!" as if I'd sneezed my sons into being.

The problem starts when I adopt this character consciously, hamming up my performance, so to speak. Egocentric Me is stroked by the positive attention ("Four boys! How do you do it?"). Lazy Me believes less will be expected of me in this role ("Tardy again, Mrs. Berry? Oh, that's all right."). I wear my drama's character as a sandwich board, a preemptive excuse for the chaos in my life. If Frazzled Mother of Four Boys is what you think of me, you'll, perhaps, overlook my messy house, filthy car, late paperwork, missing school snacks, forgotten trumpets, unanswered messages, etc.

Except, and here's the kicker, what you'll actually think of me is entirely independent of this little charade I play in my head and, furthermore, who cares what you think? This performance is staged by my ego, for my ego. It's narcissistic at its core, caring nothing for those to whom I owe honesty, friendliness, or punctual permission slips.

And it's a lie. I'm bigger and better than I let on. I'm defrauding you when I play this game. The fact is, I can manage my life better, when I choose to. The truth is, I'm making choices other than to be a better manager of all my duties. Some of those choices may be worthy, and some may not. The more I play roles to con you, stroke my ego, and appease my anxieties, the less I am looking at you, thinking about you, getting to know you, or learning to serve you.

Flat roles are invidious weeds that choke the honesty out of relationships. I've got to keep Nervous Maiden and Insecure Wifey out of the bedroom, because they sap my marriage of its potential, and focus its resources on my needs, instead of his or ours. I must keep Super Busy Young Mom out of my relationship with my own mother, lest I deprive her of the attention she deserves at this more isolated stage of her life. I've got to banish Well Intentioned But Forgetful from my friendships. Above all else, I must, must, must keep Overstressed Mother of a Herd of Hooligans out of my relationship with my sons, or heaven help them all.

Possibly the worst deception wrought by adopting shallow roles is that I, myself, come to believe in them, to accept the definitions and limitations that I've so long projected to others. This form of "losing myself" carries no prize for virtuous self-sacrifice, but only leaves me stuck and starved, pretending and powerless.

What then? Will my round bumps, my glaring self-delusions, run away with the story of my life? Am I casting myself as a supporting character, a pawn in my own existence?

This very defect is one of my psychic curves—this manipulative, self-deceptive streak of mine. I'm emotionally rotund, and convinced I can fool others into believing I'm flat.

And that, if nothing else, makes me funny.

(Round, flat...couldn't I be svelte? Is that so much to ask?)

As I write and revise the novel of my own existence, how shall I view my unruly protagonist? I can choose contempt, despair, and torn, abandoned pages. Or I can wink and nod next time I catch her pulling her shenanigans, give her a stern lecture, perhaps, and ultimately paint my heroine with empathy, amusement, and delight.

As we make the decision to dream, we are taking our lives on fully, and embracing round. We can't be flat, in part because we are being ourselves, but also because heroes aren't flat. They are real, and their lives are complex and full. If our lives are full, we are happy.

My favorite song in Macy Robison's recital *Children Will Listen* is "The Story Goes On" from the musical *Baby*. The lyrics give utterance to the raw joy I felt as I welcomed children into my world, and I think these poetic words apply to dreaming as well.

THE STORY GOES ON

So this is the tale my mother told me
That tale that was much too dull to hold me
And this is the surge and the rush she said would show
Our story goes on.

Oh, I was young
I forgot that things outlive me.
My goal was the kick that life would give me
And now, like a joke,
something moves to let me know
our story goes on.

And all these things I feel and more,
my mother's mother felt, and hers before
A chain of life begun upon the shore of some dark sea
has reached to me.

And now I can see the chain extending
My child is next in a line that has no ending
And here am I full of life
that her child will feel when I'm long gone
And thus it is
our story goes on.

—Richard Maltby, Jr.

It is my sincerest hope that a chain of dreaming begins with this book and that, many years hence, you and I will marvel at how dreaming mattered to ourselves, our families, and the world. Because we dreamed, the story—our story—goes on.

What one thing, one small thing, will you do to dream today?

ACKNOWLEDGMENTS

First and foremost, I am grateful to each one of the women whose stories are featured in *Dare, Dream, Do*—on the blog and in this book. These stories are deeply personal and it took courage to share them. Without their stories and their derring-do, *Dare, Dream, Do* would not exist. It is a privilege to have dreamed with you, the inaugural Dare to Dream girls.

Thank you to Erika Heilman and Jill Friedlander at Bibliomotion, to my agent Josh Getzler, to publicists Barbara Henricks and Rusty Shelton, to social media expert Becky Robinson, and especially to Carolyn Monaco, my book manager and mentor— you have made my dream of getting a book to market all that I could have hoped for.

I am so profoundly grateful for the encouragement and know-how of my initial Dare to Dream Team: Laurel Christensen and Jana Erickson at Time Out for Women, who in November 2009 said, "I need a book by June 2010," and then expected me to deliver; Melissa Stanton, whose early line editing and truth telling were invaluable; Vickie Sullivan, who when I first started blogging pushed me to really say something, to speak my truth; Amy Jameson, my conceptual editor, who provided everything from tough love to tactical support to sunshine; Brandon Jameson, who for over a decade has brought to life my ideas with his excellent design sensibility; and LaNola Kathleen Stone, whose photography always captures truth.

Thank you to those who were willing to review *Dare, Dream, Do.* You truly were consequential strangers, offering me just what I needed when I needed it—generosity in reading, writing, and lending your name.

And to many dear friends—including Rachael Hutchins, Julie Berry, Liz Economy, Sally Harker, Julie Marriott, Bob Moesta, Kathleen Peterson, Stacey Petrey, Macy Robison, Diane Pritchett, Lori Richards, and Jen Thomas—thank you for reading early drafts and for your willingness to walk that difficult line between criticism and encouragement. I am also deeply indebted to my lifelong friend and teacher Leslie Feinauer— thank you for daring me to dream.

Finally, I am brimming with gratitude and love for my husband, Roger, and our children, David and Miranda: you are the strawberries, sunshine, and sweetness of my life.

We only really dream when we dream together—thanks to each of you daring and dreaming with me.

ABOUT THE AUTHOR

Whitney Johnson dared to dream when she began her Wall Street career as a secretary. By her forties she had risen to become a double-ranked *Institutional Investor* sell-side analyst, a regular contributor for the Harvard Business Review blogs, and is currently the president of Rose Park Advisors, Clayton M. Christensen's investment firm. Prior to co-founding Rose Park (Disruptive Innovation Fund), Whitney was Merrill Lynch's Senior Telecom and Media analyst for Latin America, and was rated by Starmine as a superior stockpicker *vis-a-vis* her peers. When she's not picking stocks, she's taking stock in her dreams, and encouraging others to take stock in theirs, whether investing in and sitting on the boards of start-ups, keynoting industry conferences, or lecturing at Harvard Business School.

Whitney graduated magna cum laude with a B.A. in music from Brigham Young University, having played at the Montreux Jazz Festival with Synthesis, the university's award-winning big band. She was born in Madrid, Spain, is fluent in Spanish, and served a mission for her church in Montevideo, Uruguay. She and her husband reside with their two children in Boston, Massachusetts.

You can dream along with her and share the stories of your dreams at www.whitneyjohnson.com.

Twitter: @daredreamdo
Facebook: https://www.facebook.com/DareDreamDo
Pinterest: http://pinterest.com/johnsonwhitneyl